*A Tiffany Studios "Daffodil" table lamp, the fully leaded daffodil shade with long stems
that come down from a single aperture band of glass. c1900, 24in (61cm) high, A*

# Contents

## VALUE CODES

Throughout this book the value codes used at the end of each caption correspond to the approximate value of the item. These are broad price ranges and should only be seen as a guide , as prices for antiques vary depending on the condition of the item, geographical location, and market trends. The codes used are as follows:

| | |
|---|---|
| **AAA** | £100+ ($165,000+) |
| **AA** | £50–100,000 ($80,000-165,000) |
| **A** | £25–50,000 ($37,500-80,000) |
| **B** | £15–25,000 ($22,000-37,500) |
| **C** | £10–15,000 ($15-22,500) |
| **D** | £5–10,000 ($7,500-15,000) |
| **E** | £2–5,000 ($3-7,500) |
| **F** | £1–2,000 ($1,500-3,000) |
| **G** | £500–1,000 ($750-1,500) |
| **H** | £250-£500 ($400-$750) |
| **I** | under £250 (under $400) |

# Introduction

Glass is one of the few areas of antiques collecting where items are still relatively undervalued, unlike silver or porcelain. Indeed, some antique glasswares, such as 18thC and 19thC decanters, may cost only as much as a good-quality modern equivalent. For someone keen to make an investment, it is interesting to know that while a new decanter will be worth about one-tenth of its cost price once the purchase has been made, an antique will hold its value and may even appreciate over time. This book covers the most important areas of glass collecting, and follows the history of the subject from the evolution of glass production in ancient times to the highly innovative techniques of the 19thC and early 20thC. Also examined are techniques, forms and styles from glassmaking centres all over the world. Emphasis has been placed, however, on groups of items that are more accessible to the collector, including decanters, cut glass, 18thC English drinking glasses and 19thC and early 20thC glass. Pieces from these categories are both interesting and relatively affordable.

Within the field of glass collecting there is a huge variety of areas in which to specialize: a look at the different glassmaking centres is an interesting way to start.

The question of how to display a collection of glass is one that needs

*A 4thC Roman iridescent glass jug, with combed handle. 8.75in (22cm) high, G*

to be given a great deal of thought. Obviously security is a concern, but many lockable cabinets are often too dark to show items off to their best advantage. Cabinets with doors, while enabling a collection to be

*A c1st–3rdC Roman unguentarium. 3.25in (8cm) high, I*

locked away, also help to keep dust away from the glass. The appearance of glass is most effective when presented on a clear glass shelf that allows light to pass through the item. Glass is enhanced by lighting either from directly above or below, and this also serves to minimize shadows and reflection. Remember that although a bright light will emphasize colour, it may obscure tone and shape. Giving advice on buying is always difficult. Antique glass is rarely marked, and while reading the wide variety of literature available makes an excellent starting point, the only way to gain a real understanding is to handle the items themselves. Most specialist dealers will be pleased to talk you through their stock, and are a useful source of information. The larger auction houses hold viewing sessions during the week prior to a sale, and are helpful even if one has no intention of buying, because it is often possible to handle the items.

To conclude, the best way to collect antique glass is by aiming for top quality and condition, rather than quantity. It is tempting to amass a large number of less expensive pieces when starting out, but it is more rewarding in the long run to buy a single, good-quality piece using a similar amount of money.

*A 6th/7thC Byzantine glass flask, with mould-blown symbols. 5in (12.5cm) high, F*

# Types of glass

The body of a glass item is technically known as "metal". The colour and texture varies according to the ingredients. The production of clear glass, designed to imitate the mineral rock crystal, has always been a goal: the Romans made *cristallum*, and the early Venetians manufactured *vetro di cristallo* ("glass of crystal").

## Ingredients

The basic component of glass is silica, a substance that is most commonly found in the form of flint, quartz or sand. Sand will often contain impurities such as metal deposits that discolour the resulting glass: the tints in early glass can act as a guide to the area of manufacture. On its own, silica melts at a very high temperature. Adding an alkaline flux helps to bind the ingredients and reduces the melting point.

• Water-glass is a mixture of silica and sodium carbonate. Though it is similar to glass in appearance, it is soluble in water.

• Soda glass is produced by super-heating (to a temperature of over 1,000°C) a mixture of silica, sodium carbonate and calcium carbonate (in the form of chalk or limestone). Because it is relatively simple to produce, soda glass is used today to make bottles and other less expensive, disposable glass items.

• Potash glass was first made in Bohemia. Potash, or potassium carbonate, was made by burning wood and bracken from the forests, hence the German name for potash glass is *waldglas* ("forest glass"). It is hard, and is unsuitable for cutting.

• Lead crystal was developed in 1671 by British glassmaker George Ravenscroft. It used a high proportion of lead oxide to create a relatively soft, brilliant glass that was suitable for cut and engraved decoration. The proportions of the ingredients have changed slightly, but remain basically the same: three parts silica, two parts red lead, one part potash and a little saltpetre, borax and arsenic.

## Shaping glass

Ancient glass was made by winding threads of molten glass around a sand or clay core. The vessel was "marvered" or smoothed to fuse the threads together. The core was then removed. This technique was known as core forming.

The other techniques used to shape molten glass are:

• Free-blown glass, invented by the Romans in the 1stC BC, is formed from a blob of molten glass – a "gather" – that is placed on a blowing rod. Once the body has been formed, it is often transferred to a pontil rod for shaping and manipulation. On early pieces, the pontil rod was snapped off leaving a pontil mark.

• Mould-blown glass is created by blowing the gather into a mould.

• Press moulding was introduced in the early 19thC. Molten glass was poured into a mould and a plunger used to force it into all parts of the mould.

**Coloured glass**

Glass can be coloured in a number of ways:

• The entire batch can be coloured by the addition of a metal oxide.

• Cased and overlay glass comprises two or more layers of coloured glass. An outer vessel is partially inflated and a gather is then placed inside and blown, so that the layers fuse when they begin to inflate together. Strictly speaking, overlay glass describes any number of layers of coloured glass over a clear body, while cased glass is usually a clear outer layer covering a coloured body, but the terms are often used interchangeably.

• Flashed glass is made when a vessel is painted with or dipped into another colour, leaving a thin layer on the surface, which can be cut or engraved. Flashed glass is usually regarded as a less expensive version of cased glass.

• Stained glass is produced by painting a glass body with a solution of metal oxide. This can produce rich, vibrant colours, and also marbled effects if a number of different oxides are swirled on the surface of a vessel.

*An 18thC Chinese rock crystal snuff bottle, carved as a Spanish coin, probably the work of the Imperial atelier. 2in (5cm) high, D*

9

# Decorative techniques

## "In front of the kiln"

"In front of the kiln" describes hand-made decoration that takes place while the glass is still hot.

• Applied decoration is the earliest form of decoration on glass. Trailing is created by placing thin rods of molten metal on the body of a vessel, and is found on many items of ancient Roman and Egyptian glass. Many wares feature applied blobs of glass, often known as prunts, wings (commonly found on Venetian and *façon de Venise* pieces) or rings.

• Other methods include: pincering, where trailing or other applied decoration is squeezed to give a frilled effect; combing, where trailed, coloured threads are stroked or "combed" to form a wavy design; milling, where vertical grooves are impressed into the glass; wrythen moulding, where softened, vertical ribbing is swirled to encircle the glass, creating a spiral effect.

• One of the most important decorative techniques was developed in Venice in the 15thC. An opaque-white glass was invented that was named *lattimo* ("milk glass"). Used to make beakers, cups and bottles, it also formed the basis for many decorative techniques. More importantly, *lattimo* was used to create chain-effect decoration on the rims and edges of a wide variety of glassware, such as drinking glasses, *tazze* and other vessels. It could also be coloured. It is probably best known as lacy inclusions in clear glass called *filigrana* or *latticinio*, but there are many different styles, such as *vetro a fili* ("thread glass"), where the threads ran in parallel lines forming straight or spiral patterns; *vetro a reticello* ("glass with a small network"), where the threads crossed to form a lattice; and *vetro a retortoli* ("glass with a twist"), where the threads were twisted together.

## Other decorative techniques

Almost all other forms of glass decoration are produced by specialist craftsmen, usually in workshops away from the factory, and can be carried out at a much later date than the production of the vessel itself. There are five main forms:

• Enamelling is made from coloured, powdered glass mixed with an oily substance. This is painted onto the glass and reheated to fuse it.

• Gilt is gold paint, dust or leaf mixed with a fixative and then fired onto a glass vessel. Gilt decoration that is not fired is known as "cold gilding" and is less hard-wearing.

• Cutting is designed to reflect the light and make a glass object even more brilliant. It was developed principally in England, Ireland and northern Europe in the late 18thC and early 19thC. The cuts in the glass leave sharp-edged patterns in relief. The designs produced in this period comprised three main cut patterns: square-ended, "v"-shaped or hollow.

• There are three main methods of engraving glass: diamond-point, wheel and stipple. Diamond-point uses a hand tool with a diamond nib to draw lines. Wheel engraving was invented in Germany in the mid-17thC and uses a copper wheel. Stipple engraving uses a diamond needle that is tapped against the glass to create a pattern of dots. The best comes from the Netherlands. Cameo glass is made when the surface of a vessel comprising two or more layers of different-coloured glass is engraved or cut to reveal the colours underneath. The design may stand out in relief if the piece has been cased or overlaid, or may reveal

*A 1920s Gallé cameo glass vase with an amber overlay. 13in (32.5cm) high, D*

only thin layers of coloured glass if the vessel has been flashed. Invented during Roman times, the techniques have been used to create decorative wares in many glassmaking centres.

• Acid-etching involves covering the surface of a glass vessel with an acid-resistant coating, such as resin, and engraving a design through the coating onto the glass body. The glass is then dipped into acid (most commonly hydrofluoric acid), and the design is traced out by the acid giving a matt or frosted effect.

# Ancient glass

It is likely glass was first produced by the accidental presence of sand or quartz in early pottery kilns. Glass exists naturally in the form of obsidian (a glass-like rock) and pyrites (a crystalline yellow mineral), both resulting from volcanic activity. Manufactured glass seems to have first appeared in Egypt around 1500 BC, but stone beads with a vitreous glaze have also been found from as early as 4000 BC. Dating ancient glass is often a problem, and the earliest pieces that can be accurately dated bear the mark of King Thotmes III (1501–1449 BC). Other items can be dated by their similarity to various artefacts. During this period, the Egyptian army is believed to have returned with some glassmakers following a war with Syria.

Glass became an important Egyptian export, and by 331 BC the whole of the Middle East was being supplied with Egyptian wares, and some examples even reached Northern Europe. Many different forms were produced, including beakers, jugs, vases, flasks and jars. Items became more decorative, and highly coloured mosaic vessels were produced.

The Roman conquest of Egypt led to the next step forward in the development of glassmaking. Previously, Rome had been a market for Egyptian glass, but following the conquest, Egyptian glassmaking techniques were soon adopted and developed by the Romans. The major discovery was glass-blowing: this technique allowed the glass to be made more finely and evenly, and also made possible the production of larger vessels.

Political stability, established by Caesar Augustus following the defeat of Mark Antony and Cleopatra in 31 BC, allowed the glass industry to expand. Prosperity continued under subsequent leaders, and as well as working to satisfy a healthy market for luxury items, glassmakers made a full range of functional tableware in plain, undecorated glass. Both free- and mould-blown items were produced. The Romans also invented many decorative techniques, most notably cameo glass.

As the Roman Empire grew larger, glassmaking skills spread across Europe and the Near East. Glassmakers soon settled in the areas that have since become Germany, France and England, and produced wares for the Empire, but the Middle East with its abundance of raw materials was the principal manufacturer at this time.

The fall of the Roman Empire in the early 5thC BC led to the decline of the glassmaking industry, which became regionalized and isolated. All areas retained a basic Roman style but there were no longer the resources or knowledge to develop further. The Middle East, Spain, Germany, France and northern Italy had their own glassmaking areas, but for hundreds of years there were no major changes in forms or techniques.

Ancient Egyptian glass is extremely unusual and difficult to collect. Authenticity can be guaranteed only when buying from a specialist dealer or auction. While large pieces of Roman glass in perfect condition are extremely rare, smaller items are less difficult to obtain. The Romans used small glass bottles or flasks of oil when bathing, and these unguentarium were treated as disposable items. These were made in cast quantities between the 1stC BC and the 4thC AD and can be acquired relatively inexpensively. Many were also recycled: glass fragments, known as cullet, were added to the glass mix as a flux and helped to reduce the melting point, thus speeding up the glassmaking process.

Many fakes and copies have been produced. These were often not made deliberately to deceive, but have found their way onto the antiquities market, so take care when faced with an apparent bargain.

*A 1st–3rdC AD Roman unguentarium (tear bottle). 2.5in (6.5cm) high, I*

13

# British glass

Apart from some evidence of Roman glassmaking and a small amount of medieval "forest" glass made in the Weald area of England, virtually no glass was produced in Britain before the late 16thC and all supplies of glass were imported.

In 1567, Jean Carré, a glassmaker from the Low Countries, was granted a licence to make window glass and other wares at Alford in Sussex. Progress was slow, and in 1570 Carré, keen to bring the techniques of Venetian *façon de Venise* glass to England, opened a glassworks at Crutched Friars in London. He brought over a number of Italian craftsmen from Antwerp, including the Muranese glassworker, Giacomo Verzelini (1522–1606), who had lived and worked in Antwerp for 20 years. Verzelini became manager, and following Carré's death in 1572, acquired a licence to produce Venetian-style glass. The government prohibited the import of glass from Venice for the next 21 years. There are still about 12 identifiable Verzelini pieces in existence, mostly in museum collections. They are usually diamond-point engraved, and

often include a cartouche with shield, a quotation, a dedication or a date. After Verzelini's retirement in 1592, the remaining years of his patent were granted to Sir Jerome Bowes, a soldier. In 1618 Sir Robert Mansell, a retired admiral and financier, obtained control of the national monopoly. Under Mansell the glass industry produced a wide range of utilitarian wares, including wine and

*An 18thC glass goblet vase, with a fluted, rounded bowl. 10.25in (26cm) high, G*

medicine bottles, and good-quality drinking vessels. The government policy of creating a monopoly in the glass industry lapsed in the mid-17thC.

The most significant development in British glassmaking occurred in 1675, when the Glass Sellers Company employed George Ravenscroft (1632–83) to research the production of a new form of glass that, unlike Venetian *cristallo*, was not vulnerable to surface cracks or crizzling. By 1677, Ravenscroft's formula had proved successful enough to be granted a patent. His mix contained a relatively high proportion of lead oxide, between 24 and 30 per cent, and became known as flint or lead crystal. Some of his early pieces were marked with his seal, a raven's head. Lead glass was more brilliant than *cristallo*, and was softer and therefore better suited to cutting and engraving. From the late 17thC British glass developed its own shapes and styles, which set the standard for table glass throughout the world for the next 100 years.

Early 18thC lead glass tended to be very heavy, but in 1745 an Excise Act levied a tax on glass at the rate of 1d (one old penny) per pound of

*A large early English lead-glass rummer. c1720, 6in (15.5cm) high, G*

raw materials. As well as a means of generating revenue, it was also hoped that the tax would encourage manufacturers to reuse pieces of old glass (known as cullet) in the mix, which lowered the melting point and used less fuel. This left more wood available for boatbuilding and other uses. As a result, lighter styles of glassware developed, illustrated by stems with tears, twists and facets found on many 18thC drinking glasses. Drinking glasses made during this period can be dated reasonably accurately by their stems.

# British drinking glasses

The development of lead-crystal glass by George Ravenscroft at the end of the 17thC meant that the British glass industry began to flourish in its own right, and was no longer dependent on imported items and materials. It also marked the end of Venetian influence on the style of British glassware. Drinking glasses from the time took on the baluster

*A hollow mercury-twist-stemmed wine glass. c1760, 6in (15.5cm) high, I*

form that was already familiar on contemporary silverware and furniture, and there was an emphasis on strength and simplicity. Drinking glasses made in the 18thC can be dated reasonably accurately by their stems.

• The first distinctive British form was the baluster; plain, heavy balusters with knopped stems, based on a Renaissance architectural form, were made between 1685 and 1725.

• Lighter glasses, known as balustroids, and glasses with plain stems were produced from 1725 to 1750.

• Moulded pedestal or Silesian-stemmed glasses can be dated between 1715 and 1760.

• Air-twist stems were made between 1745 and 1770.

• Opaque or cotton twists date from between 1755 and 1785.

• Faceted and rudimentary (very short) stems were fashionable between 1780 and 1825.

Opaque or cotton twists are probably the most collected and easily recognizable stem form of all British 18thC drinking glasses. This form of decoration owes much to the Venetian *latticinio* and *vetro di trino* techniques of the early 17thC, where threads of white were enclosed inside clear glass. Combinations of different types of twist are unusual and valuable. Some mixed air- and opaque-twist stems were made, most of which are double series.

*An engraved facet-stemmed wine glass, on a conical foot. c1780, 6in (15.5cm) high, I*

In 1777 the glass tax in England was doubled and extended to include coloured glass, which even affected the production of opaque glass. When this was followed three years later by the granting of free trade to Ireland, where the glassmakers had previously been

*A late 18thC ale glass, on a diamond-faceted stem on a circular foot. 7.75in (19.5cm) high, G*

banned from exporting their wares, many English glassmakers moved to Ireland to escape high costs. The industry flourished, and a characteristic, high, quality, heavily cut style emerged. The 1777 Act introduced duty on coloured glass, including "enamel" glass, which meant that opaque twists became expensive to manufacture. As a result, craftsmen were forced to develop alternative decorative techniques that served to reduce the weight of glass items. The additional excise tax on glass, together with the Neo-classical style of the late 18thC, illustrated by the architecture of the Adam brothers and Josiah Wedgwood's pottery, motivated glassmakers to mass-produce cut glass. This is most commonly seen in facet-stemmed glasses. These date from 1775 to 1810 and represent the last of the distinctive stem forms of the 18thC.

# Heavy balusters

*A heavy baluster wine glass, with round funnel bowl. c1700, 7.5in (19cm) high, F*

1. Does the glass feel relatively heavy?
2. Does it have a slightly grey tone?
3. Is the base of the bowl very thick?
4. Is the foot conical or domed with a deep fold?
5. Does the stem have large, plain, well-defined knops?
6. Do the foot and bowl ring clearly when tapped?
7. Does the glass have a conical or funnel bowl (other shapes are more unusual)?
8. Is the glass free from decoration (engraving is rare)?
9. Is the surface free from crizzling?

## Early 18thC drinking glasses

Glasses known as heavy balusters were produced from 1685 to 1710.

• The lead content of the glass means it feels heavy and has a soft, grey tint.

• Heavy balusters are usually made in three pieces: bowl, stem and foot. The base of the bowl is usually thick.

• The foot is usually conical (sometimes domed) with a deep fold.

• The knops on heavy balusters are large, plain and well defined.

• Following the 1745 Excise Tax they were often recycled. This has contributed to their rarity.

### Types of baluster glass

Although all baluster glasses are rare, the largest proportion of these are goblets, but there are a number of cordial glasses with true baluster stems. Ale glasses, gins and drams are unusual.

### Knops

The knops on heavy balusters were plain at first, but by 1725 a

*A heavy baluster wine glass, on a heavy ball knop. c1710, 7in (18cm) high, E*

number of more elaborate forms had developed, including ball, cylinder, acorn, angular, bobbin, drop, mushroom and annulated. The value of a heavy baluster is determined by the rarity of the knop; the acorn is the rarest knop shape.

### Decoration

Moulded and engraved decoration is extremely rare on heavy balusters and examples valuable.

*A heavy baluster wine glass, engraved with Queen Anne's cipher. c1702, 7.25in (18.5cm) high, C*

### Size

Usually heavy balusters measure between 6 and 8in (15.5–20.5cm) tall, but there is a group of extremely large balusters. These large baluster glasses were probably made for special occasions and are rarely decorated.

Size is not an advantage in terms of value for heavy balusters: smaller pieces will always fetch a higher amount than larger ones.

# Balusters and balustroids

*A Newcastle light baluster wine glass, engraved with a coat of arms, on a flattened knop, teared knop and baluster stem. c1755, 7in (18cm) high, E*

1.  Is the stem longer than those found on heavy balusters (see pp18–19)?
2.  Does the piece weigh less than a heavy baluster?
3.  Are the knops more complex and widely spaced?
4.  Is the base of the bowl thinner than on heavy balusters?
5.  Is the piece elegant and well proportioned?
6.  If there is engraving, does it feature a Dutch subject?
7.  If stipple engraved, is the glass signed on the pontil?

## Light balusters

Lighter baluster glasses were made in the first quarter of the 18thC even before the Excise Act, as craftsmen became more experienced and were able to manipulate lead crystal with greater skill and ease. They are characterized by a wider variety of bowl shapes, including bell, thistle and trumpet, and longer, more complex stems with smaller, lighter and less-defined knop shapes.

*A Newcastle light baluster wine glass. c1750, 7.5in (19cm) high, G*

## Newcastle light balusters

Newcastle light balusters represent the highest quality of balustroids, and always have stems that are an inch or so longer than usual (about 7.5in/19cm), with exceptionally delicate knops and conical feet that are often folded. They are frequently engraved – plain examples are rare – and were said to have been shipped from Newcastle to Holland for decoration. It is now believed that they were made in Holland and decorated with diamond-point, wheel and stipple engraving.

• Common subjects include Dutch family crests, drinking scenes and ships (symbols of good luck).
• Stipple-engraved glasses are often signed on the pontil.

## Balustroids

Balustroids were made in the baluster form after c1725. More elegant than balusters, their stems are taller and thinner with fewer, more delicate knops often separated by lengths of plain stem.

## Decoration

Decoration on light balusters and balustroids, as on heavy balusters, is rare. A few pieces are engraved, usually with designs reflecting the use of the glass – such as grapes and vines for a wine glass, and hops and barley for an ale glass.

*A balustroid wine glass, engraved with foliage and floral husks. c1740–50, 8in (20.5cm) high, G*

21

# Moulded pedestal (Silesian) stems

*An early 18thC pedestal wine glass, on a four-sided pedestal stem. c1710, 7in (18cm) high, F*

1. Does the glass have a moulded pedestal stem with four, six or eight sides?
2. Does it have a conical bowl and foot?
3. If engraved, is the design a diamond-point-engraved Dutch subject?
4. Does the glass feel relatively heavy?
5. Do both the foot and bowl ring when tapped?
6. Does the metal have a grey tone?
7. Is the stem solid, perhaps with a small tear?

## Silesian-style stems

Dated between 1710 and 1750, these moulded pedestal stems became popular following the accession of the Hanoverian George I in 1714. They originated in Silesia, then part of Bohemia and now part of Poland, but have no actual link with the area. Relatively plain at first, they gradually became more decorative.

## English or Continental?

Silesian stems were made in England and on the Continent; the Continental examples tend to be half the value of English ones. English Silesian stems were made from lead crystal, the foot and bowl were free-blown, and the stem was mould-blown. The earliest and most valuable have four-sided stems. Moulded stems with six and eight sides were produced later and are less valuable. Some have odd numbers

*An early George III sweetmeat glass, with Silesian stem. 6.5in (16.5cm) high, H*

of sides, but these were probably produced by mistake. They typically have a conical bowl, a conical folded foot and feel relatively heavy. Continental Silesian stems were made from soda glass, and therefore differ from their English counterparts in the following ways:

• the metal has a duller tone
• the foot and bowl do not ring when they are tapped
• they feel light in weight
• the stems are hollow, which adds to the weight disparity caused by the difference in the metal used.

## Decoration

Some Silesian-stemmed glasses are decorated with diamond-point engraving. English engraving tends to be cruder, making it less valuable.

*A Silesian stem wine glass. c1715–20, 7.5in (19cm) high, G*

# Plain and rudimentary stems

*A mid-18thC plain-stemmed wine glass, of drawn-trumpet form with a single bead inclusion, on a conical foot. 7in (18cm) high, I*

1. If the glass has a plain stem, does it have a drawn-trumpet bowl (other shapes are less common)?
2. Is the stem tapered?
3. Does it have a tear (stems without tears are less desirable)?
4. Is the foot conical and folded (although folded feet disappeared around 1745)?
5. If decorated, is it moulded or crudely engraved with motifs such as flowers, hops and barley, or fruiting vines?
6. Is the pontil snapped off?

## Plain stems

Glasses with plain stems were made from 1730 to 1760; they were less expensive than balustroid glasses and designed for everyday use. They typically had a trumpet bowl and a folded foot, which helped protect against chipping (less common after 1745). Also common was a tapered stem with a tear, usually near the bowl. Plain stems with a drawn bowl were made in two pieces; other bowl shapes were generally made in three pieces, with a join visible between the bowl and the stem. Decoration included engraving and moulding.

*A late 18thC English dwarf ale glass, on a rudimentary knop stem. 5.5in (14cm) high, I*

## Rudimentary stems

These small 18thC glasses have very short stems, or bowls set directly on the foot. Known as rudimentary stems, they were less expensive, made for taverns and everyday use.

## Ale glasses

These were made with rudimentary stems of all types. They are usually 4–5in (10–12.5cm) tall with a conical bowl. Decoration may be engraved and "wrythen" moulded (vertical ribbing was twisted to create a spiral).

## Jellies

These glasses were used to serve savoury and other jellies. The bowls are usually about 4in (10cm) high, and frequently found shapes include pan-topped, bell, round funnel, cup and sometimes hexagonal.

## Drams

Drams are found with all 18thC stem forms, and were generally small, inexpensive glasses used in taverns to serve spirits such as gin and brandy.

*A mid-18thC plain-stemmed wine glass, with bucket bowl. 6.25in (16cm) high, I*

# Air-twist stems

*A wine glass, with drawn-trumpet bowl and double series opaque-twist stem. c1765, 7in (18cm) high, I*

1. Is the bowl trumpet-shaped (other forms are more unusual)?
2. Does the twist extend into the base of the bowl?
3. Is the twist inside the stem?
4. Is the foot folded?
5. Is the pontil snapped off?
6. If engraved, does the decoration feature an armorial, commemorative, convivial or political design?
7. Is the twist neat and well formed?
8. Is the glass good-quality lead crystal?

## Air-twist stems

Air-twist stems proliferated between 1750 and 1760, as craftsmen sought to produce lightweight, decorative drinking glasses. Early air twists were made in two pieces, with the twist extending into the bowl. They often have drawn-trumpet bowls.

## Technique

Air twists were formed by elongating and twisting air bubbles in the glass to create a pattern. The most simple form is the multi-spiral air twist, which may contain up to 12 filaments. A stem with only one style of twist is called a single series air twist.

## Decoration

Air twists sometimes feature English diamond-point engraving, which varies in quality. Stems with knops are rare: one may add 20 per cent to the value of a glass, and up to five can be found on a stem.

*A wine glass, with coarse incised-twist stem. c1760, 6.5in (16.5cm) high, G*

## Copies

Copies have been made since 1850, and those made later have ground-out pontils (on original air twists the pontil is snapped off) and flatter feet. Many were made with over-bright metal and have a white tone. They have a slightly clumsy feel, and they are often larger than 18thC originals.

## Incised twists

The incised twist was a stem form made to imitate the air twist with spiral or wrythen moulding on the outside of the stem.

*A wine glass, with double-knopped multi-spiral air-twist stem. c1750, 6.5in (16.5cm) high, G*

# Colour-twist stems

*A wine glass, with drawn-trumpet bowl and double series opaque-twist stem. c1765, 7in (18cm) high, H*

1. Is a join visible at both ends of the stem?
2. Are the twists solid and well formed?
3. Do the colours include green and/or red (blue and yellow are unusual)?
4. Is there also an opaque twist in the stem?
5. Does the bowl have a grey tint?
6. Is the bowl free from engraved decoration?
7. Does the glass ring when tapped?
8. Does it feel relatively heavy?

## Opaque twists

Opaque or cotton twists date from 1760 to 1780 and are probably the most collected and easily recognizable English 18thC drinking-glass stem form.

### Technique

The twist was made by inserting rods of white glass into clear glass, and pulling and twisting. Opaque twists were made in three pieces: the foot and bowl were moulded to opposite ends of a pre-cut stem.

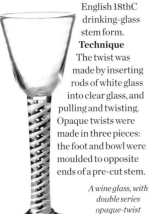

*A wine glass, with double series opaque-twist stem. c1765 7in (18cm) high, H*

## Coloured twists

Colour twists are rarer than opaque ones because coloured enamels made with different metal oxides cool at different rates, making the technique more complex. The most common colours are red and green; blue and yellow are very rare. Colour twists usually appear with an opaque twist.

## Mixed twists

Combinations of different twists are unusual and valuable. The rarest and most valuable includes all three: an air, an opaque and a coloured twist.

## Composite stems

Glasses with stems that include elements of all the popular stem types made between 1745 and 1775 are called composite stems. These combine plain sections, balusters, twists and knops. Most include a plain section and an air twist with a knop. Opaque twists in combination are extremely rare.

## Continental copies

Most colour twists are Continental contemporary copies of English pieces. They are worth a tenth of English ones. If in doubt, consult an expert, as copies and contemporary versions abound.

*A rare English colour-twist wine glass, on a short yellow, green, red and white stem. c1760–70, 4in (10cm) high, G*

# Facet-stemmed glasses

*An ogee-bowl wine glass, the diamond-cut stem with central swelling knop. c1765–75, 5.75in (14.5cm) high, H*

1. Does the glass have a flat foot with no fold?
2. Is the foot wide and fluted?
3. Is the pontil mark ground out?
4. Is the stem section hexagonal?
5. Are the facets diamond, hexagonal or straight cut?
6. Is the stem elegantly proportioned and the glass well balanced?
7. Does the bowl feature any engraving, cut or moulded decoration?
8. If engraved, does the decoration include motifs such as vines, stars, flowers, birds and insects?

## Facet stems

Facet stems date from 1775 to 1810 and represent the last of the distinctive 18thC stem forms. Following the 1777 Act the style enabled glassmakers to create attractive, lighter weight drinking glasses.

## Typical features

The development of grinding techniques in England and Ireland towards the end of the 18thC facilitated the production of faceted glasses. There are three main facet patterns: diamond, hexagonal and flat-cut. Typical features include:

*A rare, miniature facet-stem liqueur glass. c1770, 3.5in (9cm) high, H*

• A round funnel bowl: forms such as bell and trumpet bowls could not be cut very easily.
• A flat foot, which replaced the conical folded foot as the most common form.
• A ground-out pontil.
Knops are unusual on facet-stem glasses and, if found, make them more valuable.

## Decoration

The bowls of facet stems were sometimes cut with basal flutes, or featured moulded decoration such as honeycombing. Engraving was common and subjects include fruiting vines, chinoiserie, stars, flowers, birds and insects.

• There are some extremely rare English facet glasses with Dutch political stipple engraving.
• The value of a facet stem will depend on the complexity of the cut decoration on the stem and foot, and the subject of the bowl decoration.

## Copies

The Stourbridge-based company Stevens & Williams (see pp 94–5), made many facet-stemmed glasses around 1900. They can be easily confused with 18thC pieces, but the stems tend to be too thick.

*A chinoiserie-engraved facet-stem wine glass, with ogee bowl. c1780, 6in (15.5cm) high, G*

# Jacobite glasses

*A mid-18thC Jacobite air-twist wine glass of drawn-trumpet form, the stem with a pair of entwined cables, on a conical foot. 7.5in (19cm) high, F*

1. Does the glass have a drawn-trumpet bowl?
2. Is the stem plain with a tear?
3. Is there a conical folded foot?
4. Are the size and proportions of the glass similar to other early 18thC drinking glasses?
5. Does the piece feature diamond-point engraving?
6. Is there a symbolic design?
7. If there is an engraved rose, is there also a single bud?

## Jacobite glasses

In the 18thC glasses were made to support bids by descendants of James II to restore a more direct Stuart line to the throne of England. They were used for loyal toasts, which was an act of treason, and so owning one was a symbol of true allegiance.

## Jacobite symbolism

Pieces were engraved with a variety of symbols:

- Forget-me-nots, lily-of-the-valley, daffodils, a crown and oak leaves.
- Latin phrases – for example, *Redeat* ("may he return").
- The English rose was the common, and is said to represent the English crown.

*A Jacobite wine glass, the trumpet bowl on a multi-spiral air-twist stem, with folded foot. c1750, 6.25in (16cm) E*

## Amen glasses

One group of Jacobite glasses are commonly referred to as "Amen" glasses because they feature verses from Jacobite anthems, ending "Amen".

## Fakes and copies

- Copies made at the end of the 19thC are larger than the originals.
- Some 18thC glasses were engraved in the 1920s and 1930s to enhance their value. They are difficult to distinguish from genuine pieces.

## Value

All Jacobite glasses engraved during the 18thC are highly collectable, especially those made before 1745. Glasses engraved with symbols only, such as roses, are described as being "of possible Jacobite significance", and are less valuable than those that can be positively attributed.

*A Jacobite plain-stemmed, engraved goblet, with gilding. c1745, 6.25in (16cm) high, F*

# Beilby glasses

*An opaque-twist Beilby wine glass, the round funnel bowl enamelled with a vignette. c1770, 6in (15.5cm) high, E*

1. Does the glass have an opaque-twist stem (other forms are less usual)?
2. Is the foot conical?
3. Is there opaque white-enamelled decoration (coloured enamels are more unusual)?
4. Is the enamelling thinly applied and high quality?
5. Are there traces of gilding on the rim?
6. Is the piece in good condition?

## Enamelled glass in Britain

Enamelling on glass became popular in Britain c1750. By c1760 two centres had developed. The first was in Bristol, led by Michael Edkins who worked on coloured "Bristol" glass. The second, and most well known, was based in Newcastle and led by the Beilby family of seven children. William Beilby and his sister Mary are the best-known exponents.

### Beilby glasses

The wine glass opposite is a typical example. It has an opaque-twist stem, conical foot and enamelled scene.

*An enamelled wine glass. c1765, 6in (15.5cm) high, F*

### Identification

All Beilby glasses are valuable, but any attributed to William will fetch more. Few pieces were personally signed, but records were kept from 1767 until 1778.

### Patterns and designs

Early Beilby designs feature simple borders of flowers, vines and hops and barley. These were made in thinly applied white enamel and a needle was used for detail. Later, more ambitious designs include Classical ruins, pastoral subjects, landscapes and sporting scenes.

### Royal and armorial Beilbys

The most valuable pieces are known as "Royal Beilbys", and were made to commemorate the birth of the Prince of Wales in 1762. Other rare pieces include coloured armorial and commemorative glasses. Armorial Beilbys are worth ten times more than ordinary ones.

*A Beilby wine glass, decorated with a band of fruiting vine. c1765, 6in (15.5cm) high, F*

# Rummers

*An English rummer, the bucket bowl engraved with a view
of the Sunderland Bridge. c1830, 5.25in (13cm) high, H*

1.  Is the glass sturdy, with a short stem and a wide foot?
2.  Is the mouth open and not turned in?
3.  Does the glass have a capacity of 8–15fl oz (233–438ml)?
4.  Is the glass slightly grey in tone, and does the bowl ring
    when tapped?
5.  Is the pontil rough, ground out or tool marked (not machine-
    finished)?
6.  Is the inside of the bowl free from scratches?
7.  Is the base worn?

## Rummers

These 19thC goblets have short stems; the wide bowls hold 8–15fl oz (233–438ml). The name was said to be a corruption of *roemer*, a German wine glass. However, they were used for rum punch or rum and water.

## 18thC rummers

Made from around 1780, they were among the first English glasses to feature engraved decoration.

*A rummer, with slice- and flute-cut bucket bowl. c1820, 5in (12.5cm) high, I*

*An early 19thC commemorative Admiral Lord Nelson rummer. 8.5in (21.5cm) high, G*

Most were designed to be sturdy, hard-wearing tavern glasses and featured simple decoration such as a small amount of cutting on the body and foot. Feet may be cut with stars or in the "lemon-squeezer" style. From about 1810 rummers were engraved with hops and barley indicating that they were used for ale and beer. Shapes changed little as the practical nature of the glasses gave makers no incentive to experiment.

## Collecting

The relative inexpensive and robust shape of rummers make them some of the most collectable and functional items of 18thC and 19thC glass. They are highly sought after for table use. As rummers were heavily used their bases are invariably worn.

# British and Irish decanters

A decanter is used to hold a drink that has been poured from a storage vessel. They were originally intended for wines with a sediment, such as port, but the term now also describes bottles used for spirits.

Decanters made in shapes that are familiar today were first made at the beginning of the 18thC. The "shaft

*A decanter, cut with diamonds and pillars. c1840, 10.5in (26cm) high, I*

and globe" form, with a long neck and a bulbous body, extended throughout the 18thC and 19thC, and formed the basis for other shapes. The mallet decanter began to emerge during the 1720s. It had straight sides, sloping slightly outwards or inwards, with varying lengths of neck. The slope of the shoulders gradually increased and decanters were made taller; this shape became known as the shouldered decanter. Later 18thC forms include the bell (from c1750); the taper (from c1765); the barrel or Indian-club (c1775); and the "Rodney" or ship's decanter (c1780). Early decanters tended to be plain, but the rising popularity of wheel cutting and engraving during the 18thC, together with the necessity of providing lighter glass items due to the 1745 Excise Act, meant that decorated decanters became more common. Hexagonal faceting is often found on the necks and shoulders of decanters, with decorative cutting in the shape of festoons and stars on the body. Scale cutting, popular from c1760, was used on shoulders and necks. Enamelling is found on some 18thC decanters. Coloured decanters, originally made to hold spirits, were produced in the Bristol area from the 18thC onwards, in blue, green and amethyst. In the late 18thC, decanters became heavily ornamented with elaborate cut decoration, following the Anglo-Irish style. In the 19thC shapes changed in response to the revivalist periods that characterized the era. The Arts and Crafts movement of the late 19thC favoured plain, simple forms, usually with a foot.

*A Liberty & Co. Tudric pewter and glass decanter. c1900, 12in (30.5cm) high, E*

Most decanters, other than very early pieces or great rarities, are reasonably priced and often cost no more than a good-quality modern decanter, and have the added advantage of holding their value. Pairs of decanters are worth roughly three times the price of a single and are desirable. While larger sets of three or more are interesting, numbers will not dramatically increase the price. Always look for wear on the base of a decanter as a sign of authenticity.

## Seal bottles

Around the middle of the 17thC, a group of dark green (almost black) bottles developed, and these probably represented the first items of specifically "British" glassware. The bottles were free-blown, and therefore have no seam lines, they are rough on the base (the side of the pontil) and often have eccentric shapes. Used to serve wine, many are characterized by their "seal", which identified the owner when a bottle was sent back to the wine merchant to be refilled.

*A green glass wine bottle, with a circular seal beneath a crown. c1720, 8in (20.5cm) high, E*

# 18thC decanters

*A mid-18thC glass mallet decanter and stopper, engraved with a motto within a wheatsheaf cartouche. 12.5in (32cm) high, H*

1.  Is there a kick in the base of the decanter?
2.  Does the glass have a greyish tint?
3.  Is the decanter relatively light in weight?
4.  Does the decanter hold 2 imperial pints (1.1 litres)?
5.  Is the stopper a variation of the lozenge or bull's-eye design?
6.  Is it in proportion to the bottle and a good fit but not airtight?
7.  Does the texture of the stopper peg correspond with the texture of the inside of the neck of the decanter?
8.  Where there is cutting or engraving, is it relatively restrained?

## Late 17th–18thC decanters

Late 17thC decanters were made from heavy, mould-blown glass with cork or plug stoppers that were secured with string.

## Mid-18thC decanters

Taper decanters are among the earliest true decanter shapes and began to appear in the mid-18thC. They were made from lead crystal and had glass stoppers. They were usually left undecorated, although some were cut and engraved.

*A pair of Cork Glass Co. decanters, of mallet form. c1800, 10.5in (26.5cm) high, G*

Georgian decanters were not airtight and usually have stoppers that are variations of the lozenge or bull's-eye design. The texture of the peg should correspond with the inside of the neck: they will be ground or polished.

## Engraving

Decoration remained simple, although some decanters were engraved with flowers or vines. Some decoration was more elaborate, including festoons. Shouldered decanters may have engraved labels for wines such as port.

*A pair of late 18thC cut-glass decanters and bull's-eye stoppers. 11.5in (29cm) high, H*

Decanter styles evolved rapidly in the second half of the 18thC and new forms, such as applied neck rings, were produced. As well as being decorative, neck rings ensured that the vessel could be handled safely.

## Collecting

Value is enhanced by size: larger decanters are rarer and more expensive. The rarity of the shape and decoration is another factor.

# Irish decanters

*An Irish mallet-shaped decanter, with three notched annular neck rings. c1810, 10.25in (26cm) high, G*

1. Is the decanter full sized (2 pints/1.1 litres) with an ovoid form?
2. Are there moulded flutes on the base (cut fluting is less common)?
3. Does the decanter have a stopper with a moulded rim?
4. Is the rim slightly flared?
5. Are the stopper and neck polished out?
6. If engraved, are the subjects Irish, such as shamrocks and harps?

## Irish decanters

It is usually difficult to distinguish between English and Irish decanters made from 1760 to 1820 (the peak period for Irish glassmaking), but a few Irish examples are marked. This was done by blowing the glass into moulds, with the name of the manufacturer or retailer inside.

*An Irish moulded decanter, with pinched stopper. c1820, 9in (23cm) high, I*

## Marked decanters

The moulds were intended to create uniformity in shape. Unfortunately, marks imprinted by the coaster were often obscured by cutting.

• The most common maker's name is the "Cork Glass Co.", but others include "Penrose, Waterford", "B. Edwards, Belfast", "Waterloo Co. Cork" and "Francis Collins, Dublin".

• Some copies of decanters by the Cork Glass Co. were made in the 20thC; these are not engraved and have a bulge just above the fluting where they were moulded.

## Unmarked decanters

Most Irish decanters do not feature identifiable marks, but display other characteristics that mean that the piece can be attributed to Ireland. A characteristic Irish form has a slightly ovoid body, moulded fluting on the base, milled neck rings and a stopper with a moulded rim. The stoppers are always polished in and frequently do not fit very well. A double neck ring (where they appear there are usually three) is typical of the Belfast area. Another characteristic is a flared lip; damage to this will detract from the value.

### Size

All Irish decanters occur in full (2 pints/ 1.1 litre) or half (1 pint/570ml) sizes, but marked examples seem only to be full sized. No magnum decanters can be attributed to Ireland.

*An Irish club-shaped decanter, with a pair of neck rings. c1800, 9.75in (25cm) high, H*

# Regency decanters

*A Regency decanter,
with a diamond-cut
band. c1810, 9.75in
(25cm) high, I*

1. Does the decanter feel relatively heavy in weight?
2. Does it have a large body and a short neck?
3. Does the glass have a grey tone?
4. If there are rings on the neck, are they applied to the outside of the bottle?
5. Is there heavy-cut decoration?
6. Does the decoration include flutes and/or diamond cutting?
7. Does the decoration on the stopper match the decoration on the body of the decanter?
8. Is the decanter in good condition?

## Regency decanters

The fashions of the Regency period (1811–1820), when George, Prince of Wales (later George IV) ruled on behalf of his father George III, were popular until c1840. In the glass industry, 18thC gilded and engraved decoration was replaced by heavy cutting. Regency decanters show the extent of the glass cutter's skill.

## Cut-glass decanters

Initially, the Regency style featured horizontal bands or panels of deeply cut motifs such as relief or strawberry diamonds.

Flat cutting in vertical flutes was introduced c1825. Pillar cutting, where the glass was cut into round flutes to imitate pillars, was the most expensive form as a large amount of glass was required.

Matched pairs can fetch up to three times as much as single decanters. Sets of more than four are rare.

*A William IV decanter, cut with prismatic steps. c1835, 14in (35.5cm) high, G*

*A decanter, diamond and flute cut, with blown stopper. c1830–5, 10in (25.5cm) high, I*

## Stoppers

The stoppers of Regency decanters are often cut and are usually variations of the mushroom stopper, although other shapes are found, such as the ball and bull's-eye. The quality of the cutting and the metal are important determinants of value.

## Beware

• Condition is important. The glass should have a soft grey tone; brown or yellow tints due to impurities in the mix should be avoided.
• A genuine Regency decanter should be worn on the base through use.
• Continental copies usually have a brown tint and non-British features such as heavily cut bases. Continental copies are worth only two-thirds as much as an original.

# Victorian decanters

*A shaft and globe decanter, scale-cut neck, lens-, flute-, and diamond-cut body, with hollow blown stopper. c1860–70, 13in (33cm) high, I*

1. Is the decanter a shaft and globe shape (other forms are less common)?
2. Is the neck the same length as the body?
3. Does the decanter have a 2-pint (1.1-litre) capacity?
4. Does the decoration on the stopper reflect the decoration on the body?
5. Is the decoration architectural in style?
6. If cut or engraved, does the design include motifs such as stars, ferns and fruiting vines?
7. If the stopper and the body are numbered, do they correspond?
8. Does the glass have a grey tone?
9. Is the decanter in perfect condition?

## Victorian decanters

Decanters dating from about 1840 were influenced by late Georgian and Regency styles, but were more elaborate. Their form was architectural with pointed stoppers and flamboyantly shaped bodies. They often featured mixed styles of cutting and bands of engraving. Some have "Gothic" arches and spandrels.

*A set of 19thC glass decanters in a stand. 14.5in (37cm) high, H*

## Shaft and globe decanters

The most common Victorian decanter was the shaft and globe, with a round body and a neck that is about the same length. Most had a capacity of 2 imperial pints (1.1 litre), although those made towards the end of the 19thC held the equivalent of a modern bottle (750ml). Victorian decanters are relatively common so they must be in mint condition to have any value.

## Stoppers

The stoppers usually reflect the decoration on the body. Some later shaft and globe decanters have faceted ball stoppers.

## Novelty decanters

The Victorians loved novelties and this passion can be seen in a number of animal-shaped decanters, like the one below. They often feature silver or silver-plated mounts.

## Fakes and copies

Some later styles are still being made and may be confused with older pieces. The colour of the body on early shaft and globe decanters will have a grey tone, but on later pieces the glass will appear almost as bright as on modern versions. If there is a manufacturer's mark, it is likely the item is 20thC or later.

*A late 19C novelty silver-plated walrus decanter. 14in (37cm) long, F*

# Arts and Crafts decanters

*A James Powell & Sons, Whitefriars sea green decanter, with silver stopper, probably designed by Harry Powell. 1905, 10in (25.5cm) high, F*

1. Does the decanter have a simple, thinly blown form?
2. Does it feel relatively light in weight?
3. Is the glass clear?
4. Has the clarity of the glass been emphasized, perhaps by the addition of a foot?
5. If there is decoration, has it been added by hand?
6. Does the decoration on the stopper match the decoration on the body?

## The Arts and Crafts Movement

In the second half of the 19thC a group of artists, craftsmen and designers developed a new ideology. It was based around two principles: a rebellion against mass-market, machine-made items, and an appreciation of the dignity and serenity of the Middle Ages. Followers believed forms should emphasize the true beauty of glass. Decoration was restrained and should be carried out by hand "in front of the kiln".

## Designers and manufacturers

One of the firms that worked most closely with the Arts and Crafts Movement was James Powell & Sons of Whitefriars, London. The decanter shown opposite illustrates

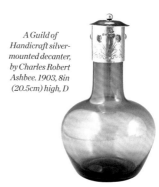

*A Guild of Handicraft silver-mounted decanter, by Charles Robert Ashbee. 1903, 8in (20.5cm) high, D*

*A Liberty Cymric silver-mounted decanter. c1903, 10in (25.5cm) high, D*

Arts and Crafts principles, with a simple, clear, thinly blown functional form, and is light in feel and appearance. Other designers who applied Arts and Crafts principles to decanters and other glass designs were Archibald Knox, with his Cymric range for Liberty & Co. in London, and Charles Robert Ashbee's pieces for the Guild of Handicraft in the Cotswolds.

## The Venetian influence

The Venetian style was also an influence on the new design ideology, especially when Venetian glassmaker Antonio Salviati opened a London showroom in 1868. British firms responded by producing Venetian-inspired pieces with applied ribbing, festooning and *filigrana*.

49

# Art Deco decanters

*A 1930s Stuart enamelled decanter and matching glasses, decorated with a geometric pattern in alternating acid-etched and plain columns. 10.5in (26.5cm) high, H*

1. Can you see marks from the seams where the glass was blown into a mould?
2. Was the decoration acid-etched or cut into the glass? Or was it produced by a mould?
3. Is there a signature?
4. Is the decoration geometric or highly stylized?
5. Is any enamel decoration in good condition?
6. If the decanter is part of a set, does the decoration on all the pieces match?

## Art Deco decanters

After the First World War, the demand for glass in new, modern styles grew. Factories responded to this, making pressed, cut and enamelled decanters. Signed pieces fetch a premium but expect to pay more for an unsigned example that epitomizes the Art Deco style.

*A Keith Murray for Stevens & Williams (Royal Brierley) cut-glass decanter. c1935, 9in (23cm) high, I*

*A Monart decanter, with stopper. c1930, 8.5in (21.5cm) high, F*

## New technologies

Factories used the latest mould-blowing and acid-etching techniques to create affordable glasswares. Similar techniques were used by glass artists at Lalique, Daum and Schneider in France; WMF in Germany; and Steuben in the USA.

## New designs

Art Deco decanters often feature bands of geometric patterns, such as the cut and enamelled example shown on page 50. Other popular decoration includes exotic Egyptian or African patterns, or stylized flowers, leaves or female figures. These designs may be cut or etched into plain, clear or coloured glass or into cameo glass, or enamelled onto a plain surface. French designer Maurice Marinot designed marbled and mottled glassware. His influence can be seen in the mottled glass created by Schneider and Daum in France (often as the ground for cameo glass), and pieces such as the Monart range developed at the Moncrieff Glassworks in Scotland.

51

# Early claret jugs

*A Regency cut-glass claret jug and stopper. c1820, 9.75in (25cm) high, I*

1. Does it have a narrow neck like that of a decanter?
2. Is there a low handle?
3. Is the cut decoration typical of the period?
4. If there is a stopper, does it match the style of the jug?
5. Does the stopper fit the jug or is it loose (which may mean it is a replacement)?
6. Is the glass free from damage?

## Wine and claret jugs

From the 18thC, meals in grand houses included a selection of wines chosen to complement the food. A number of items were developed to assist, including jugs, decanters, funnels, coasters, wine tasters and wine labels. Wine and claret jugs exist in silver from the mid-18thC and in glass from the end of the 18thC.

*A fine glass ewer, with prism and diamond cutting. c1810, 9.75in (25cm) high, G*

In general, wine was bought in casks and the head butler would pour it into a jug before the meal. As glass manufacturing developed in the early 19thC, wine began to be sold in bottles and, at the same time, glass serving vessels became more numerous as the burgeoning middle classes began to consume more wine and required the same accoutrements as the upper classes.

## Early claret jugs

Early claret jugs did not have a stopper or cover but they can usually be distinguished from water jugs because they have a narrow, decanter-type neck. However, some were made with a wider neck to help the wine to breathe before it was served. Generally, claret jugs were made with a low handle to make pouring easier.

Early glass claret jugs feature similar decoration to other glass items made at the time: hobnail and prism cutting, such as that shown on the ewer on the left; slice cutting and neck rings, as seen on the claret jug below; and plain or cut-glass stoppers similar to those on the jugs shown opposite and below.

*A claret jug, with three neck rings, slice cutting to shoulders and base, with hollow blown stopper. c1830, 10.5in (26.5cm) high, H*

# Victorian claret jugs

*An early Victorian silver-gilt-mounted claret jug, Reilly and Storer, London. 1849–50, 11.75in (30cm) high, E*

1. Does it have a pouring lip and a high, looped handle?
2. Is the stopper taller than the top of the handle?
3. If it has a silver mount, is it silver-plated or solid silver?
4. Is the glass secure within the mount?
5. Is the plaster holding the glass in place stained?
6. Does any hallmark on the lid match the date on the mount?
7. Is there any damage to the glass under the silver?
8. Does the glass fit snugly into the mount around the pouring lip?

## Victorian claret jugs

The most commonly found claret jugs were made in the mid-19thC. Many are identical to decanters but they have a pouring lip, a high, looped handle and a stopper that is taller than the handle. Coloured jugs were used to serve white wines or champagne, or were decorative.

*A Christopher Dresser claret jug, by Hukin & Heath, designed c1880. 7in (18cm) high, D*

## Dr Christopher Dresser (1834–1904)

Dr Christopher Dresser, a Scotsman, trained as a botanist, but he became a designer in the early 1860s. Early examples of his work are always plain with silver or electroplated mounts, but this style proved so popular that many variations were produced.

## Silver-mounted wine jugs

Silver-mounted jugs first appeared c1860. Most early examples are silver-plated, but from 1880 to 1914 solid silver examples were common. Silver-mounted glass is sought after.

### Collecting

• Check that the plaster holding the mount onto the glass is secure.

• If the plaster is stained and dark it may need replacing.

• If hallmarked, check that the date on the lid matches the mount.

• Check for damage under the silver because the glass around this area is vulnerable.

• Ornate silver mounts will increase the value.

• Check that the glass fits snugly into the mount around the pouring lip; if it does not it could be a replacement.

*A silver-mounted cut-glass claret jug, London. 1867, 12in (30.5cm) high, G*

# English and Irish cut glass

Cut decoration was first used in the 1stC BC and examples of Roman and Islamic cut glass exist. The skills seem to have been lost cAD 1000, and cutting was not used widely until the early 17thC in Bohemia. Methods developed rapidly and production spread across Europe.

Cut glass first appeared in Britain at the end of the 17thC, but no examples

*A George III silver-gilt-mounted cut-glass skep and dish. 1800, 5.25in (13cm) high, F*

have survived and it is probable that the majority of cut glass found in Britain during the first 20 years of the 18thC was imported.

By the early 18thC, British lead crystal had been developed that was softer and less brittle than its Continental counterpart, and was better suited to the cutting process. The development of cut glass in England was hampered by the 1745 Excise Act, which encouraged the production of thinner glass that was less well suited to cutting; the Act did not apply to Ireland, and a thriving glass industry became established there. Cut glass was produced by Irish and English craftsmen in Ireland in the late 18thC and early 19thC, and a style of glass developed known as Anglo-Irish.

Cut glass was produced by all major English manufacturers in the 1820s and 1830s, including W. H., B. & J. Richardson, Thomas Webb & Sons and Apsley Pellatt. Broad, flute-cut Regency-style glass was popular at this time. After 1840, diamond cutting was reintroduced, and by the time of the Great Exhibition of 1851, following the repeal of the Excise Tax on glass in 1845, highly elaborate cut designs were being produced reflecting a new era of industrial prosperity. F. & C. Osler was the leader in this field in terms of the quality of its pieces.

*A Regency cut-glass urn and cover, the body cut with diamonds. 6in (15.5cm) high, H*

There are four main processes in cutting. First the pattern is drawn onto the blank glass. Then the main lines of the pattern are rough-cut into the glass using a power-driven (first by the feet or water, then steam, now electric) iron wheel. The wheel is flat, curved or "v"-shaped, depending on the cut required.

The third process involves smoothing the glass using a variety of sandstone wheels. The accuracy of the cutting relies on the skill of the craftsman: one of the most obvious signs of poorly cut glass is small inaccuracies, particularly on the base, where all the points may not meet in the centre. The final, and most time-consuming process, is polishing: a wooden wheel with a fine abrasive surface is worked over the cut lines, and is often finished with a felt wheel. Polishing gives a final shine to the piece. From the beginning of the 20thC it has usually been carried out by acid-dipping, which removes a minute layer of glass from the surface and leaves a bright finish. However, the uniformity of the surface, with no wheel marks, can have a flat, bland appearance, which lacks the sharpness of hand-finished glass.

*A Victorian cut-glass goblet, with an etched cricket scene. c1850, 5.5in (14cm) diam, E*

# Cut-glass bowls

*A late 18thC Irish cut-glass oval bowl, with a shaped rim and flared moulded foot and small rim chips. 13.5in (34cm) wide, F*

1. Are there two or more different types of cutting (single styles are more unusual)?
2. Is the stem short and sturdy?
3. Is the foot a square-cut "lemon-squeezer" shape (other forms are more unusual)?
4. Does the bowl have a slightly irregular shape?
5. Does the glass have a pale grey tone?
6. Does the design appear regular and complete?
7. If there is a "lemon-squeezer" foot, are the edges smooth?

## Cut-glass bowls

Bowls were typical of the luxury cut-glass items produced in Ireland between 1780 and 1835. Many bowl forms can be clearly attributed to the Irish glassmaking industry. Three main shapes developed towards the end of the 18thC: the canoe or boat shape, the kettledrum and the turn-over rim. Bowls were made mainly as decorative pieces for the dining table.

*A pair of early 19thC cut-glass and gilt-metal campana wine coolers 7.75in (19.5cm) high, E*

*A pair of early 19thC Irish Regency cut-glass covered urns. 12in (30.5cm) high, F*

### Boat-shaped bowls

The cutting on boat-shaped bowls is often more ornate on the rim. Stems are usually short and sturdy. The "lemon-squeezer" foot is common.

### The kettledrum

Kettledrum bowls were often larger than other forms, and commonly featured bands of two or more different types of cutting. Sometimes the rims were left uncut. Kettledrum stems are usually short and sturdy, occasionally with a simple knop, and the feet are plain and round.

### The turn-over rim

Bowls with a turn-over rim were the most difficult to manufacture and the most expensive. Turn-over rims always have "lemon-squeezer" feet. Many Irish pieces were slightly lopsided, and the metal was slightly grey in colour (more so than the usual lead-crystal tone), possibly due to impurities in the mix.

### Collecting

• Bowls that measure more than 11in (28cm) high and 15in (38cm) long will be worth slightly more than smaller examples.

• The functional nature of bowls means that they are often scratched; those that are least scratched are the most desirable.

# Cut-glass cruets

*George III sterling silver six-bottle cruet stand, by Paul Storr, London.*
*1810 and 1811, 11.75in (30cm) wide, E*

1.  Does the set feature two bottles, two bottles and three casters, or more pieces?
2.  Are all the bottles the same height?
3.  Are all the pieces made in the same style, with the same decoration?
4.  Are all the hallmarks similar?
5.  Do the pieces fit the frame?
6.  Does the glass fit snugly inside the silver mounts?
7.  Is the set complete and with no damage?

## Cut-glass cruets

Cruets – silver-mounted glass vessels for serving condiments at the table – were first used at the end of the 17thC when oil and vinegar were introduced as flavourings to be added to food at the table.

*A George III cruet frame, with eight cut-glass bottles. 1808–9, 9in (23cm) high, E*

The decoration of the bottles and stand reflects contemporary fashions and many are made from cut glass. Early sets feature two glass bottles (for oil and vinegar) with silver mounts, but by the 1720s they included three covered casters for sugar, pepper and mustard. These are often referred to as "Warwick" cruets. The bottles and casters were held in a silver frame, which had decorative feet and a handle. By the 19thC the number of bottles had increased to include soy and other exotic sauces. The set might include serving spoons and silver labels for the bottles.

## Collecting cruets

Smaller items such as cruets were produced in vast quantities, making it relatively easy to build a collection. All the bottles within a set should be the same height and the glass should fit the mounts with no movement.

When buying, check that all the silver parts feature a similar hallmark (any different marks suggest a replacement piece) and that there is no damage, especially under the silver where the glass is more vulnerable.

*A large early Victorian silver "Warwick" cruet. 1838–9, 15.25in (39cm) high, B*

# Glass lighting

Glass lighting has been produced for centuries; the most notable early examples are probably glass shades for a group of mosque lamps made in the Middle East in the 12th–14thC. The commercial production of glass lighting started in the late 17thC following the development of lead crystal, and had begun to flourish by the end of the 18thC.

Up until the end of the 19thC, candles provided the main source of artificial

*A George III bell-form hall lantern, with cylindrical glass shade, later fitted for electricity. 33in (84cm) high, G*

light and candlesticks were made in a number of materials, ranging from wood to precious metal. Lead-crystal glass provided the ideal medium for candlesticks because of its reflective qualities, and it could be made thick and clear, or heavily cut. They were usually made in pairs in order to magnify the production of light by reflecting off one another. The shapes of candlesticks broadly followed the fashions of the stems of 18thC drinking glasses, but were also influenced by styles of furniture. Multi-branched candlesticks, or candelabra, developed from the candlestick. These too were luxury items that tended to be used in the main rooms of large houses. They were extremely fragile with many delicate parts.

The reflective qualities of cut glass were utilized further by the development of lustres, which were cut-glass prisms attached around the candle or other source of light. The edges of the drip pan or sconce would be pierced, and long, cut-glass drops would be hung from it.

Chandeliers are not the most efficient form of glass lighting, but are the

*A pair of 19thC gilt-brass and cut-glass candlesticks, with lustres. 13in (33cm) high, H*

most impressive. The production of chandeliers is highly skilled and the work is extremely intricate: a medium-sized chandelier usually has several thousand parts. Originally intended to hold candles, chandeliers were modified to use gas after the 1830s, when metal gas pipes were incorporated into the branches. They are now powered by electricity, and glass arms have been reintroduced. Glass has also been used as covers or shades for lamps, to protect the source of light from draughts, wind and rain, and was especially important for lights used outside.

Glass was not usually used to cover a flame entirely, because direct heat tended to cause the glass to crack; instead, glass covers protected the sides of the flame. When glass covers were used they were fixed well above the heat. Shades for candles – glass tubes that fit around the flame – were also made in Britain.

Glass lighting is a relatively expensive area of antique glass collecting. It is important to remember that items such as chandeliers and wall lights are often sold by furniture dealers and at furniture auctions rather than by specialist glass dealers or at glass sales. Pairs of candlesticks, lustres and wall lights are worth three to four times the price of a single piece; this does not apply to most central lights or chandeliers, but pairs of hall lanterns are desirable.

*A 20thC bronze and glass hall lantern. 52in (132cm) high, G*

# Candlesticks

*An early 18thC George III glass candlestick, the turned stem
raised on a folded lobed circular foot. 8in (20.5cm) high, G*

1.  Does the candlestick have a popular 18thC stem form?
2.  Is it made from high-quality lead crystal?
3.  Does the candlestick feel relatively heavy?
4.  Is the foot wide, heavy and possibly domed and terraced?
5.   Is the stem knopped?
6.  Does the candlestick measure 8–10in (20.5–25.5cm) in height?
7.  Is it in good condition?
8.  If the candlestick is straight and sconced, is there a (removable)
    pan to collect the wax?

## 18thC candlesticks

In the 18thC glass candlesticks were relatively uncommon, and silver, being less expensive, was more widely used. Made from around 1730, they were luxury items, often made in the same forms as drinking-glass stems. Air twists were made from 1750 to 1760, opaque and colour twists from 1760 to 1775. While 18thC glass candlesticks are 10–20 times more rare than drinking glasses with similar stem forms, they are only two or three times more expensive.

## Facet-stem candlesticks

These are more common than other forms, and were made between 1740 and 1880. As a result, pieces are difficult to date accurately.

*A late 19C James Powell & Sons, Whitefriars glass candlestick centrepiece. 14in (35.5cm) high, F*

## Taper candlesticks

Taper candlesticks are identical in form to other 18thC candlesticks but are small, usually no more than 4in (10cm) high (candlesticks usually measure 8–10in/20.5–25.5cm high), and have very fine stems.

They were usually produced singly, unlike full-sized candlesticks, which were generally made in pairs.

## Collecting

• Pairs will be worth four times the value of singles (apart from tapers).

• Be wary of later facet-stem candlesticks, which may not be made from crystal and are over-shaped.

• Examine a piece carefully for damage: cracks caused by heat are quite common.

*A pair of 19thC Regency-style candlesticks, with diamond-cut stems. 10in (25.5cm) high, G*

# Candelabra and lustres

*A pair of possibly Irish cut-glass candlestick lustres, with hollow vase-form stems cut with repeat lozenge motifs. c1800, 8.75in (22cm) high, G*

1. Is the candelabra made from a mixture of materials?
2. Do all the glass pieces match (for example, colour and style of cutting)?
3. Is the candelabra well proportioned?
4. Is there a glass bead at the top of each drop?
5. Are all the drops in place?
6. Is there a finial at the top (such as a crescent or a pineapple)?
7. Is the candelabra easy to dismantle?

## 18thC candelabra

Throughout the 18thC the terms "lustre", "branch" and "girandoles" were used interchangeably to describe all kinds of glass lighting – ranging from a candlestick to a hanging chandelier. But by the end of the 18thC, "candelabra" came to mean a multi-armed candlestick. The earliest examples date from about 1750. The arms usually slotted into a brass plate at the top of the base and could be lifted out for cleaning.

*An early Victorian cut-glass and gilt-brass candelabrum. 12in (30.5cm) high, H*

## Lustres

The term "lustre" is used to describe a candlestick with a drip pan from which rods of faceted glass are suspended to catch and enhance the light. In fact "lustres" are the glass drops hanging from the drip pans. The long, flat cuts on lustres will

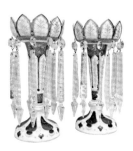

*A pair of mid-19thC green opaque cased-glass lustres. 11in (28cm) high, E*

maximize the production of light, and small beads attached to them help the lustres to hang more easily and allow some movement, adding to the overall effect.

## Victorian candelabra

The Victorian tendency for over-decoration saw highly ornate and coloured pieces being produced.

• Clear glass candelabra are more collectable than coloured pieces.
• A pair is worth four times as much as a single candelabra.

## Condition

• Check that all the drops are present – replacing them can be expensive.
• Redundant holes in the base suggest an alteration or something is missing.
• There are usually an even number of arms so it should look balanced.

# Chandeliers and lanterns

*A Victorian cobalt-blue glass chandelier, with six scrolled branches and hurricane lamp shades, with gilt accents and hung with prisms. 37.5in (95cm) high, E*

1. Do all the elements match?
2. If a chandelier, is there an even number of arms?
3. Are the body and arms correspondingly ornate?
4. Is the plate to which the arms are attached free from holes?
5. Is the chandelier well balanced?
6. If damaged or reconstructed, are the changes minor?

## Chandeliers

Chandeliers have been made for hundreds of years from brass, wood, iron and, more rarely, silver, but glass has only been used since the mid-18thC. They were show pieces and are impressive and expensive.

## 18thC chandeliers

On early 18thC pieces, the centre column was often made from a series of spheres, and the branches emanated from further down the stem. By the late 18thC the branches were fixed around the middle of the column, usually in two layers. Various numbers of lights could be used;

*A pair of late 19thC Adam revival ormolu and glass hall lanterns. 24in (61cm) high, E*

unwanted lights were replaced by arms with decorative finials.

As chandeliers were often damaged, a degree of replacement is acceptable. Major reconstruction and composite chandeliers should be avoided.

## Lamps

Ceiling lights were designed to hold candles and subsequently oil lights. They were made with narrow frames to create as much light as possible. The value of hall lanterns lies in the framework. The original glass will add value, but replacement glass will not greatly affect the price. Many lights have been converted to electricity: a sympathetic conversion can add to value.

A huge variety of wall lights were made, from miniature chandeliers to simple glass and brass cages.

*mid-19thC silver-plated cut-glass chandelier, wired for electricity. 45in (114.5cm) high, E*

# 19thC – early 20thC British glass

A huge variety of glasswares were produced in Britain during the 19thC. The benefit of high-quality lead-crystal glass, together with a supply of low-cost labour, meant that craftsmen were able to experiment with new techniques. A growing middle class generated a demand for all kinds of decorative arts. Victorian glassware often exhibited a tendency towards over-ornamentation, but many new forms and styles emerged. The series of international industrial exhibitions in the mid- to late 19thC raised the profile of glassworkers and designers, providing the opportunity for contact between them and a number of potential employers. Marking glass did not become common until the early 20thC; even at the end of the 19thC factory marks were rare, though the artists occasionally signed their work. Many major modern glasshouses were established and thrived during this period, while several older factories and glassmaking centres declined because they failed to innovate, such as the Irish glassmakers.

Many British factories were particularly influential, such as W. H., B. & J. Richardson, Thomas Webb and Stevens & Williams (now Brierley). The scale of these glassworks gave their craftsmen both the opportunity and the resources with which to experiment, and significant developments were made in this way.

Developed in the United States in the 1820s, machine-pressed glass was not mass-produced in Britain until the Excise Tax on the weight of glass was repealed in 1845. Many factories started to make

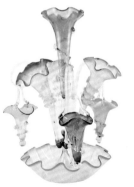

*A Victorian multicoloured glass epergne. 18.5in (47cm) high, I*

*A 19thC Edward Varnish & Co. flash-cut glass goblet. 7in (18cm) high, G*

pressed glass, and a large number of decorative, functional and inexpensive wares were made. There was a revival in the production of cameo glass in the 19thC. In 1786 the famous Roman artefact the Portland Vase, a white-on-blue cameo, had been brought to England by the Duke of Portland. Many glassworkers attempted to copy the vase, and Benjamin Richardson, a Stourbridge manufacturer, offered a prize of £1,000 to the first person who could make an exact replica. The process was so complex that a successful copy was not completed until 1876: John Northwood carried out the carving on a blank made by

Philip Pargeter, the owner of the Red House Glassworks in Stourbridge; the whole operation took three years. The production of cameo glass in the 19thC was facilitated by the introduction of a technique known as acid-etching. This process used acid (usually hydrofluoric) to eat away at the surface of the glass, and was used to create matt or frosted designs as a form of decoration on its own, but was also used in the preliminary stages of cameo cutting to save time. For the collector there is a huge range of wares available, but as a result condition is all-important. Prices vary to suit every pocket. The most valuable items are usually those that have taken the most time to produce.

*A 1930s Jobling "Dancing Girl & Block" centrepiece. 9.5in (24cm) high, I*

# Nailsea glass

*A Victorian Nailsea glass bell, with Bristol blue bell and moulded yellow glass handle. 9.25in (23.5cm) high, I*

1.  Does the bell have a coloured, probably decorated body?
2.  Does it have a clear handle (coloured ones are more unusual)?
3.  Is the handle knopped?
4.  Is the bell in two pieces with a plaster of Paris join?
5.  Does it have a clapper, or a wire hook for a clapper?
6.  Does the glass have any applied decoration?
7.  Is the piece made with obvious skill?
8.  Does it have purely decorative value?

## Nailsea glass

A generic term for decorative pieces made by glassworkers, for their own profit and sometimes for apprentice tests or guild processions, from the glass left at the end of the day. The Nailsea Glasshouse, near Bristol, established in 1788, made bottle and crown window glass.

*A Nailsea glass transparent ruby and clear rolling pin. c1880, 12.5in (32cm) long, I*

Nailsea items were made in Bristol and the surrounding area, and include bells, such as the one shown opposite, flasks, walking sticks, ships, birds of paradise and pipes, and were popular between 1850 and 1900. Nailsea-style decoration describes the looped trails of opaque white or coloured glass found on many of these pieces.

### Bells

These are the most frequently found Nailsea items, usually with clear handles and coloured bodies, although more than half are red. Bells with coloured handles, such as the one shown opposite, are very rare. The handles and bodies were made as two separate pieces and joined with plaster of Paris. There is often a wire hook embedded in the plaster to take a clapper. Bells with clappers do not tend to be more valuable, although they may be more desirable. Some copies were made in the 1950s. These tend to be very ornate, and the glass tends to be coarser and thicker.

### Other Nailsea glass

• Flasks and pipes usually feature combed, looped or striped decoration.
• Sailing ships made of filigree glass were made in the Midlands.
• Rolling pins were made from the early 18thC onwards, first in crown glass and later coloured.

*A Nailsea glass wall pocket. c1880, 8in (20.5cm) high, H*

# George Davidson & Co.

*A very rare Davidson "Orange Cloud" glass flower dome, in "modified" orange. 1931–5, 11in (28cm) diameter, H*

1. Does the piece bear a mark of a crowned lion rampant over battlements?
2. If there is a registered trademark, does the number correspond with Davidson's pattern books?
3. If pearline glass, is it one of the colour ranges produced?
4. If "Red Cloud" glass, does it have painted undersides?
5. If "Orange Cloud", are the trails a custardy-yellow (original orange) or darker ("modified" orange)?
6. If Cloud glass, is it from one of the colour ranges produced by George Davidson?

## George Davidson & Co. (1867–1987)

Built as the Teams Glass Works in Gateshead in 1867, George Davidson & Co. initially manufactured chimneys for oil lamps. Decorative ware was introduced in 1878. George Davidson died in 1891 and his son Thomas took over the company.

### Decorative glass

Thomas Davidson introduced one of the company's most famous productions, Pearline glass, which went from clear to opaque. Patented in 1889, blue was the first colour introduced, followed by the acid yellow known as "Primrose", often called "Vaseline" glass by

*A Davidson "Good Companion" lamp. 1936–58, 14in (35.5cm) high, H*

collectors, and the clear "Moonshine". Cloud glass was introduced in 1923. Darker trails of glass are mixed with a lighter colour, which, when moulded, produces unique patterns. The first colour was purple, followed by blue, amber, red, orange and green.

The production of Cloud glass mostly ended before the Second World War. "Amber Cloud", which was by far the most popular colour, continued to be sold into the mid-1950s. In the late 1950s Davidson introduced a new shade, "Topaz-Briar" (a bluish-brown), for a short period. "Orange Cloud" and "Red Cloud" were mainly produced for export and are the rarest colours.

*A pair of Davidson "Blue Cloud" glass tall candlesticks. 1925–34, 7.5in (19cm) high, I*

# Sowerby

### Sowerby (1807–1972)

Sowerby began to make glass about
1807 in Gateshead, near Newcastle.
Although it made decorative
pressed glass from the 1840s, it is
the pieces made from the 1870s and
1880s onwards that this factory is
remembered for.

*A 1930s Sowerby "Ladye Pot" powder puff
pot in lime green. 6.6in (17cm) high, I*

*A 1930s Sowerby "Squirrel Bowl"
centrepiece, amber. 8in (20.5cm) high, I*

The factory was under the direction
of John George Sowerby from 1871,
who adapted designs by Walter Crane
and other designers to produce
Arts and Crafts-inspired pieces.
Vitroporcelain was introduced from
1877. This opaque glass was created
to give the appearance of porcelain,
but was much cheaper to produce.

The colours included a white, "Opal",
a blue, "Turquoise", and an ivory
called "Queen's Ivory Ware".
By 1880, Sowerby produced glass
in new colours such as "Malachite"
(often called "slag" glass), "Drab
Green", "Giallo" (yellow), "Gold" and
"Blue Nugget" were added, joined by
"Tortoiseshell", "Rubine" (deep red
translucent) and "New Marble Glass"
(like brown malachite) in 1882. The
firm continued to innovate in the
1920s and 1930s and closed in 1972.

### Marks

The Peacock trademark was used
from 1876 until 1930.

# Jobling

### Jobling (1886–1949)

James Augustus Jobling acquired Greener & Co. (see p79), in Sunderland, in 1886, but also ran into financial difficulties. Things began to change under the management of his nephew Ernest Jobling-Purser who was appointed in 1902.

Through investment in new machinery the firm began to grow, but it was the acquisition of the licence to produced PYREX ovenproof glass in 1921 that established Jobling on a more successful footing.

*A Jobling Art Deco-style-handled "Celery" vase. c1934, 7.75in (19.5cm) high, I*

*A 1930s Jobling Jade "Statue & Block" centre-piece, by Franckhauser. 13in (32cm) high, I*

With the success of the PYREX range, the firm began to produce art wares. Launched in 1932, its art glass ranges sold well and included the popular Jade glass.

After initially attempting to seek a licence from Lalique and Sabino, Jobling produced its own pieces in a similar style. Opalique, an opalescent glass reminiscent of Lalique, was registered as a trademark in 1935, earlier pieces being marked "Reg. No. Applied For". Jobling's Opalique figures and rarer plaques are sought after and considered to be some of the best British pressed glass of its era.

77

# Other pressed glass

For centuries, glass was the preserve of an elite. While the Industrial Revolution of the 18thC moved glassmaking into towns and cities,

it remained a mainly handmade product until the early 19thC. This began to change in the United States following the invention, in 1825, of press moulding, a mechanized method of glass production.

The innovation was soon adapted in Europe and was particularly popular in Britain. The main British centres of production were the North East of England and the Midlands.

*A late 19thC uranium yellow posy vase, by John Derbyshire. 9in (23cm) high, I*

*A late 19thC Burtles Tate & Co. pressed glass swan posy in opalescent pink. 3in (7.5cm) high, I*

### Derbyshire (1858–93)

Various members of the Derbyshire family operated glassworks in Salford, Manchester, from the 1860s until 1893. The firm's products are valued for their quality and inventiveness. Unlike its main rivals, Sowerby and Davidson, Derbyshire produced figurative pieces. They are often marked "JD" with an anchor.

*A green Bagley & Co. "Andromeda" centrepiece. 12in (30.5cm) diam, I*

### Burtles, Tate & Co. (1858–1924)

Established in 1858 in Manchester, this small factory initially produced a variety of domestic wares. But it is remembered by collectors for its "Swan" and "Elephant" posy holders (see left) introduced from 1885.

## Greener & Co. (1858–85)

Based at the Wear Flint Glass Works in Sunderland, Greener produced fancy and commemorative wares. Henry Greener originally worked for Sowerby (see p76) and established his own firm in 1858 as Angus & Greener. The glassworks used two main trademarks: from 1875 to 1885

*A Greener amethyst glass target ball. 3in (7.5cm) high, H*

this was a demi-lion rampant facing left, holding a five-pointed star in its right paw, and between c1885 and 1900 a demi-lion holding a battleaxe in both paws.

*A 1930s British blue shoe-shaped, pressed glass thimble holder, with silver-plated thimble. 1.75in (4.5cm) high, I*

## Other makers

Many factories produced mould-pressed glass, which was not marked

*A Victoria Golden Jubilee pressed glass and engraved dish. 1887, 8.5in (21.5cm) diam, I*

and so its maker is often impossible to identify even if it has been marked. These mass-produced pieces were often inexpensive copies of cut-glass designs, which appealed to the growing middle classes, novelties (such as the thimble holder, below) and commemorative pieces (including the dish, above). Other recorded factories include Hepple (1874–84), based in Newcastle. It mainly produced industrial glass, but made fancy wares from 1874 until the firm's closure in 1884 when its moulds were bought by Davidson. Among Hepple's products were coal-scuttle-shaped sugar bowls and models of colliery trucks.

# Cranberry glass

*A Victorian cranberry glass epergne. 20in (51cm) high, H*

1. Is the colour a paler shade rather than a deep ruby?
2. How old is it? Look for wear; 19thC examples will have a worn, matt, "ring" of wear to the base where they have been in contact with the surface of a table or shelf.
3. Does it feel light? Later pieces, particularly reproduction examples, tend to weigh less.
4. Is there any damage? Crimps and frills, often associated with cranberry wares, can shear and chip easily. Also check for cracks around handles of jugs and baskets.

## Cranberry glass

The term "cranberry glass" is a relatively modern one, but has stuck as it describes this attractive shade of

*A Victorian cranberry glass jug, gilded and hand-painted. c1870, 4in (10cm) high, I*

glass well. Cranberry is a later and paler version of "ruby glass", which has been prized by collectors for centuries.

Deep red glass was known in Roman times, but the technique for making it was lost and not rediscovered until the mid 17thC, when glass makers discovered that adding gold oxide to glass and then slowly cooling it created a deep, intense ruby colour. The high cost and complex nature of making ruby glass meant that it

remained an elite product until the mid-19thC.

In the mid-19thC, there were improvements in glassmaking techniques; in particular, gas-fired ovens as well as new methods involving less costly ingredients. This meant that the production of cranberry glass took off.

In Britain most cranberry glass was made by glassworks in Stourbridge. In the USA it was made by various glass factories including the Boston & Sandwich Glass Co. (pp186–7).

## Fakes

This market is plagued by fakes or modern versions. Look for wear. Older pieces will be heavier.

*A Victorian art glass vase, with applied blossom decoration. 1.25in (2cm) high, I*

# Bristol glass

*An early 19thC blue wine-glass cooler, signed I. Jacobs, Bristol. 2.5in (6.5cm) high, G*

1. Is the glass blue or green (other colours are less common)?
2. If a bottle, does it have a capacity of 1 imperial pint (570ml)?
3. Is the body free from cut decoration?
4. If a decanter, is there gilded decoration on the stopper and body of the decanter?
5. Does the body have a gilded label identifying the contents, and the stopper the first initial?
6. Does the gilding have a smooth, "old" gold matt finish?

## Bristol glass

The term "Bristol" encompasses all blue, green and amethyst glass made in Britain from the end of the 18thC until the middle of the 19thC. In fact, only a

*A rare Bristol blue glass decanter. c1800, 10in (25.5cm) high, G*

small group of gilded blue items are known to have been made in Bristol. These include pieces signed I. Jacobs, Bristol. Isaac Jacobs worked as a gilder in Bristol in the late 18thC and early 19thC.

## Spirit bottles, decanters and cruets

Decanters or spirit bottles, most commonly made in blue, were often gilded with a label identifying the contents: rum, brandy or Holland (gin). Stoppers are often gilded with the first letter. Bristol decanters are generally pint-sized; larger ones are rare. Eighty per cent of decanters are blue and green. Many Bristol cruet bottles were made in decanter form and decorated in a similar way.

## Drinking glasses

The most common colour for Bristol drinking glasses is green, and they were meant to hold port rather than wine. They were made in a huge variety of shades.

Bristol drinking glasses are about 4in (10cm) high. Common bowl shapes are the drawn trumpet, drawn funnel and tulip. Stems are usually plain.

• Amethyst drinking glasses are rare and usually have drawn-trumpet bowls. The colours are delicate and show no trace of red when held up to the light; Victorian copies have a plum colour when tested in this way.

• A large number of blue drinking glasses were made during the first half of the 20thC. Generally, these are larger and have unusual shapes and a very thin body.

• Green glass disappeared after c1850.

## Value

Late 18thC Bristol glass is rare and expensive, but later pieces are affordable.

*A mid-18thC Bristol green wine glass, probably gilded in the atelier of James Giles. 4.25in (11cm) high, I*

# Kerosene oil lamps

*A 19thC oil lamp, with a column moulded with Art Nouveau-style flowers. 26in (66cm) high excluding funnel, G*

1. If it is a bowl type, does it have a short stem and two short handles?
2. If it is a bowl type, does it have two tubes and a central hole for filling it with oil?
3. Does the lamp have a base, reservoir, shade and chimney?
4. Is the decoration similar on all sections of the lamp?
5. Do the sections fit together well (if not they may be replacements)?
6. Are there any chips or scratches?

## Early oil lamps

Rooms were lit by lamps that used oil and a wick from Roman times. In the 13th–14thC, enamelled and gilded mosque lamps were made, and elaborate Venetian glass lamps were used in the 16th–17thC. By c1680 modest glass lamps were being used in European homes. These featured a wick that floated in a bowl of whale oil. These generally featured a short stem and two short handles. Similar lamps were used in the USA in the mid- to late 18thC. They usually had two tubes for two wicks and a central hole for filling the lamp.

*A 19thC oil lamp, with shade etched in the Greek Key pattern. 30in (76cm) high, G*

## 19thC oil lamps

The elaborate glass oil lamps associated with 19thC interiors were variations of the "Argand" lamp. It was developed by Aimé Argand in Switzerland in 1784, and subsequently manufactured in France, Britain and the USA.

*A pair of late 19thC brass and cut-glass-mounted columnar table oil lamps. 36in (91.5cm) high, G*

19thC lamps feature a tubular hollow wick, covered with a chimney and fed with oil by a tube from a reservoir. This ensured a plentiful air supply, which in turn ensured that the oil burned quickly, producing a bright light. Once the wick was lit, it burned for as long as there was oil in the base. The level of illumination could be altered by winding the wick up or down using a pin positioned on the side of the lamp.

## Styles of oil lamp

19thC lamps were made in many styles, including Art Nouveau (such as the example shown opposite), cast brass with a pottery base (as shown above) and Classical brass designs with glass globes etched in a Greek Key pattern (shown on the left). Small, portable lamps were used to light the way from room to room rather than light every room.

# Scent bottles

*A mounted glass scent bottle, with a screw cover and cut decoration, Birmingham marks. c1880, 2.75in (7cm) high, I*

1. Is the bottle well made and carefully finished?
2. Does the glass body feature cut or gilded decoration?
3. If coloured, is the body blue, green, opaque white or (occasionally) amethyst?
4. Does the scent bottle have a metal cap made from silver or silver gilt, that fits over a glass stopper?
5. If there is a metal cap, does it screw onto the bottle?
6. Is the glass stopper airtight?
7. If the stopper is not metal-topped, is the top the same colour as the body of the scent bottle?
8. Is the bottle in good condition?

## 18thC scent bottles

The first British scent bottles were made at the beginning of the 18thC. They followed European designs and were flat in shape, but had British features such as heavy, lead-crystal bodies with cut decoration.

*A Victorian double-ended scent bottle, with brass mounts. c1870, 5.75in (14.5cm) high, H*

British-style scent bottles began to be made in the mid-18thC in a variety of colours including blue, white, pale green and occasionally amethyst. They were often made in pairs to go inside a travelling case: one for perfume and one to hold smelling salts. Pairs of scent bottles are valuable, and those with cases are worth even more.

*A Victorian silver-gilt cage-work scent bottle, in a fitted case. 3.5in (9cm) high, F*

## 19thC scent bottles

Some Victorian scent bottles copied popular gothic shapes. Many 19thC scent bottles were coloured; later ones were often made with silver mounts. Flamboyantly decorated bottles were imported from Europe, and mounts added by the retailer.

• Late 19thC scent bottles often have hinged lids; earlier examples tend to have screw-on caps.

• Double-ended scent bottles have one section for perfume and another for smelling salts, with a different fastening device for each end.

*A Victorian egg-shaped bottle, with silver-plated bird's head stopper. 1.5in (4cm) long, I*

## Cameo scent bottles

The revival of cameo glass in Britain at the end of the 19thC stimulated the manufacture of elaborate scent bottles by the firms of Thomas Webb and Stevens & Williams. Webb employed skilled cutters, including George and Thomas Woodall.

# W. H. Richardson

**W. H. Richardson (1842–1930)**
William Haden Richardson and later, brothers Benjamin and Jonathan, were involved in a number of glassworks in the Midlands from the early 1800s. The factory became W. H., B. & J. Richardson in 1842.

*A W. H. Richardson jug, typically with no pouring lip. c1860–70, 6.25in (16cm) high, H*

The firm, which was now based in Wordsley, produced high-quality glass, supplying high-end shops as well as the royal family. It used many patented techniques, including Bohemian-style glass with panels that were alternately flashed with coloured glass and left clear, and then decorated with engraving.

**Vitrified Colours**
Another famous Richardson patent was known as "Vitrified Colours". Items with this technique were displayed at the Great Exhibition in 1851. This involved transfer-printing and firing a black or coloured pattern onto the glass body. Sometimes the enamels were hand-painted onto the body although this is less common.

**Cameo**
Richardson produced high-quality cameo glass, employing artists such as John Northwood, who famously copied the Portland Vase.

*A pair of 1850s W. H. Richardson goblets, with water lilies. 6.5in (16.5cm) high, F (each)*

# James Couper & Sons

## James Couper & Sons (1855–1922)

The firm of James Couper & Sons was established in 1855 in Kyle Street, Glasgow, and produced a wide range of glass. Today it is best known for its Clutha glass range (named after the old Celtic word for the river Clyde), which was introduced in 1888 and made until c1905.

*An 1890s James Couper & Sons green glass solifleur vase, designed by Dr Christopher Dresser. 19in (48cm) high, E*

Clutha glass tends to be transparent pale green, yellow or amber, and it often contains bubbles, aventurine inclusions (small "gold" flecks) or swirling coloured trails.

## Designers

Some of the best Clutha pieces were created by eminent Victorian designer Dr Christopher Dresser. Pieces marked as a Dresser design, or ones that can be attributed to him, bring a premium. Not all Clutha pieces are by Dresser.

Some are known to be by architect and designer George Walton, and examples by Walton are beginning to be appreciated more by collectors; other examples are by unknown designers. The Clutha mark alone doesn't necessarily mean a piece can be attributed to Dresser or Walton. Many of Dresser's shapes are similar to his designs for Linthorpe pottery and seek inspiration from South American or ancient forms.

The glass was used to line pewter wares designed by Archibald Knox and sold by the Liberty & Co. store in London.

## Marks

Clutha glass usually bears a large etched mark, which often occupies the whole of the base. Arranged around a lotus flower, are the words "Clutha" often with "Registered" or "Reg Trade Mark", some pieces also bear the words "Designed by C.D. for Christopher Dresser".

*An 1890s "Clutha" bottle vase, by Dr Christopher Dresser. 11.75in (30cm) high, E*

# James Powell & Sons

*A James Powell & Sons solifleur vase, with aventurine
inclusions. c1901–10, 4in (10cm) high, H*

1. Is there a pontil mark? Powell glass was always free-blown or
   blown into moulds, never machine-made.
2. Is the item heavy? Rarely marked, handmade Powell glass will
   seem relatively heavy when compared with more commercial
   glass.
3. Does it have innovative colours? These typify Powell's work. Look
   for distinctive shades such as "Straw Opal" and "Blue Opal".
4. Is the object of high quality? Powell's products are well designed.

## James Powell & Sons (1834–1980)

James Powell & Sons was one of Britain's longest-running and most innovative glassmakers, and was closely allied to the Arts and Crafts Movement. It dated back to the 18thC, and took over a glasshouse off Fleet Street in London in 1834.

*A 1920s James Powell & Sons Whitefriars vase, by James Hogan. 9.5in (24cm) high, I*

### Stained glass

In its early years it was known for stained glass production, particularly for mass-produced, moulded, printed and stained "quarries", the individual sections used to make stained glass windows. These proved popular during the 19thC boom in church building, but are now rare, as most of these windows were later replaced. From the middle of the 19thC, domestic wares were introduced.

### Henry James Powell

Further innovation was initiated when James Powell's grandson, Harry James Powell, joined in 1875. An Oxford chemistry graduate, his experiments introduced new and previously unattainable colours as well as heat-resistant glass. By the turn of the 20thC, Powell's was one of the world's leading glassmakers. In 1923 the firm moved from central London to Wealdstone, near Harrow, to the west of London. The period between the World Wars was one of continued innovation for the company, now named Powell & Sons, with stylish Art Deco pieces that used optical moulding and dramatic cutting to great effect.

*A James Powell & Sons Whitefriars Minerbi service decanter, by Harry Powell. 1906, 9in (23cm) high, G*

91

# Whitefriars Ltd

*A Whitefriars glass large "tear" vase, designed by Barnaby Powell. c1935, 10.5in (26.5cm) high, G*

1. Check the colour of the glass. Whitefriars colours are distinctive. Are they correct? Check the right colour for the ranges.
2. Is the piece comparatively heavy? Genuine pieces will feel heavy.
3. Is there a pontil mark? Whitefriars pieces are hand-blown and will have a polished pontil mark on the base.
4. Is the shape from a known Whitefriars range?

## Whitefriars Ltd (1834–1980)

A glassworks was founded at Whitefriars, just off London's Fleet Street, in the 17thC. In 1834, London vintner James Powell purchased the Whitefriars glassworks (see pp90–1). Powell & Sons was involved with the Arts and Crafts Movement and worked with William Morris. The period from the 1920s up to the Second World War saw Whitefriars move towards a more modern style.

### Designers

Many of the new designs for the now named James Powell & Sons (Whitefriars) Ltd were created by

*A Whitefriars gold-amber glass vase, by William Wilson. 1935–7, 12in (30.5cm) high, H*

*A Whitefriars vase, with a double-ribbed neck and applied drops, designed by Barnaby Powell. c1935, 12in (30.5cm) high, H*

Barnaby Powell, the great-grandson of James Powell. Powell returned to the board of directors in 1928 and it is probably from this time that he became the principal designer. He

was joined by James Hogan in 1932 and William Wilson in 1933, who transferred from the ailing stained glass department. James Hogan's son Edmond also created some designs, mainly cut Art Deco patterns.

### Styles of wares

During this period the principal design elements were colour, cutting and shape. Typical pieces were the "Wave-ribbed" designs produced from the 1920s, which saw moulded forms such as ruched curtains enhance vases, and "Streaky", which originally saw blue, amber, ruby and green mixed to great effect. The Streaky range was clearly influenced by the stained glass department.

93

# Stevens & Williams

*A tall Stevens & Williams silver-mounted claret jug.*
*c1895, 14in (35.5cm) high, E*

1. Is the piece marked with a fleur-de-lys and "SW"?
2. If it looks Japanese in style, does it have RD 15353 engraved, making it Mat Su No Ke?
3. If it is in Keith Murray's style, is it signed with his facsimile signature?
4. Is it heavy? Like all handmade pieces, Stevens & Williams pieces will seem relatively heavy.
5. Is there a registration mark? Many of the firm's ranges were registered and may only bear this number preceded by "Rd".

## Stevens & Williams (1847–1926)

Established in 1847 in Stourbridge, Stevens & Williams produced high-quality and heavily cut crystal glass

*A 1930s Stevens & Williams vase, designed by Keith Murray. 11.75in (30cm) high, F*

in traditional and popular styles. This began to change from 1881 with the appointment of Frederick Carder, followed in 1882 by John Northwood as manager and art director. Under Northwood's direction, Stevens & Williams began an intense period of innovation in design and techniques. Among these were Mat Su No Ke glass, a Japanese inspired range; Jewell Glass; Verre de Soie; Tapestry and Moss Agate; all of which pushed technical boundaries. Steven & Williams also created high-quality cameo glass, the best of which were engraved by Northwood himself.

## Royal Brierley (1926–present)

Despite Northwood's death in 1902, and Carder's departure in 1903, Stevens & Williams prospered and received a Royal Warrant in 1919. The company changed its name to Royal Brierley Crystal in 1926 and continued to produce innovative designs. Many of these were by the New Zealand-born architect Keith Murray (1892–1981) who was employed on a freelance basis from 1932 to 1939. He created more than a thousand designs, but examples were made in small quantities, sometimes as low as six. Royal Brierley went bankrupt in the late 1990s, but the name is still used in association with Dartington, under the control of US conglomerate Enesco Inc.

*A 1930s Royal Brierley "Streamline" cut-glass vase, by Keith Murray. 10.25in (26cm) high, G*

# Thomas Webb & Sons

*A cameo Chinese-style double-gourd vase, carved by F. Kretschman and coloured by Jules Barbe. c1888, 10in (25.5cm) high, A*

1. If cameo glass, is it marked "Gem Cameo"?
2. Is the piece marked "WEBB CORBETT"? This is another firm (see pp100–1)?
3. If in Queen's Burmese style, is it marked?
4. Have you looked closely for a mark? The acid-etched script "Webb" mark can be small, and with scratching to bases, hard to find.
5. Is it a high-quality piece?

## Thomas Webb & Sons (1837–1990)

Established in the glassmaking centre of Stourbridge by Thomas Webb (1802–69), who was later joined by his sons, the company was one of the best British makers of high-quality glassware. It is best known for its cameo, Queen's Burmese ware by John Northwood (1836–1902) and Thomas and George Woodall, and its rock crystal-style glass.

Following the death of Thomas Webb in 1869, the company passed to his son, Thomas Wilkes Webb, and it is under his direction that much of the

*A "Gem Cameo" vase. c1900, 7.5in (19cm) high, G*

*An unsigned Webb cameo vase, with floral and foliage design. c1900, 9.5in (24cm) high, F*

firm's fame was found. The quality and craftsmanship of Thomas Webb & Sons' work was recognized when

Thomas Wilkes Webb was made a Chevalier of the Legion of Honour, one of France's highest decorations to be awarded to a foreigner.

### Designers

As well as having its own team of craftsmen, Webb also employed freelance glass decorators, such as the French gilder and enameller Jules Barbe, who came to Stourbridge from Paris in 1879. Barbe often worked in the fashionable Oriental style using raised paste goldwork.

Dependent on the complexity of the design, Barbe's pieces could take many weeks to create.

# Thomas Webb wares

### Rock crystal

The rock crystal technique was developed by William Fritsche and first referred to by name in 1878. Using deep cutting, wheel engraving and polishing, it imitated expensive, carved, natural rock crystal. Another Bohemian engraver, Frederick Engelbert Kny, worked on this technique, which may have been created as a collaboration. This style

*A late 19thC Queen's Burmese scent bottle, gilded by Jules Barbe. 5in (12.5cm) high, G*

*A rock crystal vase, engraved by William Fritsche. c1880, 8.25in (21cm) high, D*

of work was done by other makers with the best examples marked or sometimes signed by the artists.

### Queen's Burmese

This opaque yellow/pink glass was patented in America by the Mount Washington Glass works in 1885. Thomas Webb gained a licence to manufacture it in 1886.
Made using uranium oxide and gold,

the pink colour appears when the glass is reheated; the intensity of the pink tint varies with the amount of heat applied. Mainly seen with a satin finish, non-satin pieces are rare.

*A white and cranberry glass vase, on three feet. c1890, 7.75in (19.5cm) high, I*

A favourite of Queen Victoria, the name supposedly derives from her having likened the colour to a Burmese sunset.

*An eagle's head scent bottle, gilded by Jules Barbe. 1884, 7in (18cm) long, E*

## Cameo

Developed in the 1870s by John Northwood, the cameo technique was inspired by the famous Portland Vase in the British Museum and by ancient carved stone cameos. It is created by casing one or more layers of glass in another colour and then cutting back the outer

*A 1930s "Cameo Fleur" vase, signed "Webb". 8in (20.5cm) high, I*

layer to create a design. Webb's best pieces are marked "Gem Cameo" and occasionally retailer marks such as "Tiffany of New York", with whom Webb exhibited in Paris in 1889. Brothers George and Thomas Woodall created many of the best pieces, including plaques and vases of exhibition quality. George Woodall signed some of his best works.

*A 1930s cut and acid-etched vase, similar to "Cameo Fleur". 8in (20.5cm) high, I*

### Cameo Fleur

This was a later development of Webb's cameo technique. It was introduced in 1929 and in production throughout the 1930s. Sometimes wrongly called "pseudo cameo", it was a technique that "cut" the glass by means of chemicals rather than carried out by hand.

# Webb Corbett

**Webb Corbett (1897–1969)**
Not to be confused with Thomas
Webb & Sons (see pp96–9), Webb
Corbett was established in 1897

*A cut-glass vase, by Irene Stevens, decorated with circles and bands. c1950, 11in (28cm) high, H*

by Thomas and Herbert Webb
(grandchildren of Thomas Webb),
and George Harry Corbett.
**Wares and designers**
The company specialized in cut and
engraved glass as well as enamelled
pieces. Webb Corbett's enamelled
ranges often feature fruits and
flowers, and have a translucency
reminiscent of stained glass. Its
Agate Flambe range made during
the 1920s imitated polished agate.
Webb Corbett produced rock

crystal-style pieces similar to those
of Thomas Webb. Many of these
were designed by William Kny
(1870–1942), who was the son of
Thomas Webb's famous designer
Frederick Engelbert Kny. During
the 1930s, Kny introduced more Art
Deco-style designs to the range.
Perhaps the most interesting
designer working at the factory was
Irene Stevens, who joined in 1946.
She favoured bold, simple cutting,
which can often give an abstract look,
similar to the work of Keith Murray;
her pieces are highly sought after.
Stevens left to pursue a teaching
career in 1957. Acid-etched marks or
foil labels can sometimes be found.

*A late 1940s clear cut-glass vase, by Irene Stevens, unmarked. 8in (20.5cm) high, J*

# John Walsh Walsh

**John Walsh Walsh (1850–1951)**
Businessman John Walsh Walsh
entered the glassmaking business
in 1850 when he bought into an
existing concern in Birmingham's
Winson Green area. Walsh died in
1864 and his business, including the
glassworks, was put on the market.

*An intaglio-cut and engraved "Gay Ware" bowl,
with floral design. c1935, 10in (25.5cm) wide, I*

*A 1930s cut-glass vase, marked "Walsh
Birmingham". 6.5in (16.5cm) high, H*

The glassworks was bought by one
of his daughters, Ellen Eliza, and her
husband Thomas Ferdinand Walker.
**19thC production**
The firm produced a wide range of
well-designed, high-quality goods
such as vases and flower holders,
lamp shades and table glass. The
firm specialized in flower holders for
dining tables, which were often based
on flowers such as roses, honeysuckle,
tulips and waterlilies. Novelty was
very much part of its repertoire, with
items such as horseshoes or owl-
shaped flower holders. The factory
also made cut-glass decanters, wine
glasses and fruit bowls.
**20thC wares and designers**
During the 20thC, cut glass
dominated Walsh's production.
In the 1930s, cut glass with an Art
Deco aesthetic was designed by
Clyne Farquharson (1906–72)
who had joined the firm in 1924.
Farquharson's cut-glass designs are
considered to be among the most
striking and original British cut-glass
designs of the 1930s.
The "Koh-i-noor" design was a deeply
cut pattern that was to be a flagship
product, in production until 1951.

# Stuart & Sons

*A 1920s cut-glass vase, by Ludwig Kny, acid-etched mark.*
*7in (18cm) high, F*

1. Is there a mark? Look for acid-etched "Stuart", often with an RD number or "Stuart ENGLAND".
2. If a table glass, does it have a characteristic 24-star cut to the foot?
3. If enamelled, is it a spider's web or devil design?
4. Is it signed? Some of Ludwig Kny's enamel pieces are signed "L Kny".
5. If cut glass, is the quality good?

## Stuart & Sons (1883–2001)

Frederick Stuart began working at the Red House Glass Cone at

*A late 1930s vase, with outlined horizontal bands. 7in (18cm) high, H*

Wordsley, near Birmingham, in 1827 aged 11.

### 19thC production

An 1876 directory listed the factory's products as "cut glass chandeliers, lustres, wall lights, hall lights, engraved, etched & ornamental glassware". In 1887 the factory patented "medallion Cameo" glass. Differences with his partners caused Frederick Stuart to take on the lease himself in 1882, forming Stuart & Sons in 1883. During the latter part of the 19thC and into the 20thC, Stuart was well known for producing table glasses and cut-lead crystal.

### 20thC wares and designers

The factory is best known for its 20thC fine-quality, clear cut glass. The Bohemian engraver Ludwig Kny (1869–1937) produced extremely modern designs from 1918 to 1937. His designs were the firm's mainstay. He also introduced a range of enamelled wares such as cocktail shakers and vases. These were either outline printed and coloured by hand or free-hand decorated. Kny was followed by Reginald Pierce and John Luxton. Stuart & Sons Ltd took over Strathearn Glass in 1980 and produced mould-blown art glass as well as its cut glass.

*A 1930s vase, designed by Graham Sutherland, with acid-etched mark. 6in (15.5cm) high, F*

103

# Other Art Deco glass

## Monart (1924–61)

Monart glass was made at the Moncrieff Glassworks in Perth, Scotland. The factory initially made industrial items until Isabel Moncrieff, the wife of the factory's owner, encouraged Spanish glassblower Salvador Ysart to develop a range of art glass. The name "Monart" was a composite of Moncrieff and Ysart.

*A 1930s Monart lamp and shade, with swirling inclusions to the rim. 22in (56cm) high, E*

Ysart and his sons designed over 300 shapes between 1924 and 1933. Production ceased in 1939 and was resumed on a smaller scale after the war under eldest son, Paul Ysart. Most pieces were free-blown. The glass gathers were rolled in brightly

*A 1930s Monart glass vase, with cylindrical neck. 10in (25.5cm) high, F*

coloured crushed enamel and then coated in a layer of clear glass before being blown into shape. Different-sized flecks of enamel produced a wide variety of mottled effects. Monart pieces have a distinctive ground pontil mark.

## Vasart (1947–65)

After the Second World War, Paul

*A Vasart vase, two-toned pink body with pink and blue swirls. c1947–64, 10in (25.5cm) high, I*

Ysart, his father and two of Paul's brothers set up Vasart to produce glass that tends to be paler in colour and less widely collected than Monart today. Their specialities were vases, bowls, miniature baskets and paperweights. Ysart Bros. became known as Strathearn Glass in 1965. The company was acquired by Stuart & Sons in 1980.

## Gray-Stan (1926–36)

The Gray-Stan factory was founded by Elizabeth Graydon-Stannus in Battersea, London. It made handmade glass designed to celebrate creativity and artistic freedom.

While the glass was influenced by factories such as Monart, but had a distinct identity. Pieces are signed "Gray-Stan" or "GRAYSTAN BRITISH".

*A 1930s Gray-Stan mottled glass vase. 7.5in (19cm) high, I*

## Hartley Wood (1836–1989)

The Wear Glass Works – later Hartley's – was founded in Sunderland, England, by brothers James and John Hartley. The firm closed in 1892 but that year

*A 1930s spherical pink mottled Nazeing lamp base. 6.25in (16cm) high, I*

*A 1930s Hartley Wood "Antique Glass" vase. 12.5in (32cm) high, I*

James Hartley's grandson, James Hartley Jnr, founded a new company with some of the original company's staff.

The name changed to Hartley Wood & Co. in 1895 when Alfred Wood, the leading colour mixer from Hartley's, joined as a partner. During the 1920s and 1930s Hartley Wood was known for decorative glass with streaky colour combinations that were known as "Antique Glass".

## Nazeing Glass Works (1928–present)

In the 1920s and 1930s the Nazeing factory in Nazeing, Broxbourne, Hertfordshire, produced hand-blown decorative coloured glassware. Wares included vases, baskets and bowls in mottled coloured glass. Applied handles and feet were made from clear glass. Marks include an acid-etched "NAZEING, MADE IN ENGLAND" or paper labels.

# Stained glass

In the Middle Ages, monastic workshops and later guild workshops made decorative windows from coloured glass. Pieces of stained or enamelled glass were held together with lead strips in an abstract or figurative design. It was typically set in an iron framework and used as a window.

*An Aesthetic Movement panel inscribed "Music". 27in (68.5cm) high, F*

The glass was coloured with metallic oxides to produce colours such as blue, green, gold and brown. Drapery, features and other decoration were then painted onto the

*A late 19thC panel of Greek goddess Thalia, by Arthur Louis Moore. 44in (112cm) high, F*

surface before it was fired. This technique was used for some of the finest 13thC and 14thC stained glass cathedral windows. From the late 15thC into the 16thC, stained glass windows were typically rectangular

*An Art Nouveau panel depicting two maidens. c1900, 84in (214cm), E*

panes of clear glass painted with coloured enamels.

The art of stained glass was largely abandoned in the 17thC and 18thC, but it was revived in the 19thC with the Aesthetic Movement and the Gothic Revival, and due to the influence of William Morris (1834–96) and the Pre-Raphaelite painters. Among the artists and designers creating stained glass at this time were Arthur Louis Moore (1849–1939), Charles Edward Kempe (1837–1907) and Ernest Archibald Taylor (1874–1951). Stained glass windows, doors and panels were common features in Art Nouveau and Art Deco interiors. They were incorporated into the design of many homes. Some were set into screens that could be positioned

*A late 19thC "Gather Ye Rosebuds" panel, by Charles Edward Kempe. 45.5in (115.5cm) high, E*

to make the best use of the sun's light, while others were positioned to take advantage of the natural light. While many were made by famous designers and architects, many more were made by unnamed factories and craftsmen.

In Scotland, Charles Rennie Mackintosh (1868–1928) used glass panels to highlight the "light feminine" and "dark masculine" nature of his interiors for commissions such as the Ingram Street Tea Rooms in Glasgow. There,

*A landscape panel, by Ernest Archibald Taylor. c1910, 6.75in (17cm) wide, F*

visitors glimpsed the room through a glass panel before entering it. Alphonse Mucha (1860–1939) the Art Nouveau Czech painter, poster-artist and designer, also designed stained glass and featured the flowing-haired woman used in his posters as the focal point.

In New York, Tiffany & Co. produced panels and screens for domestic interiors, before adapting the technique for its lampshades.

*A Scottish School panel, depicting stylized plant forms. c1910, 24in (61cm) wide, H*

# 18thC–20thC French glass

The history of the French glass industry dates from Roman times. Glassmaking was already a thriving industry in Rome, and as the Empire expanded, Roman glassmaking knowledge spread across Europe. Made from the ashes of ferns or bracken, the first French glass, known as *verre de fougère* or "forest glass", was amber or pale green in colour. It closely resembled German *waldglas*. The industry operated on a small scale until the Middle Ages when a demand arose for decorative glass windows; most were made for churches, but later for large houses. Venetian forms influenced local glass production, and very little "French"-style glass was made during the period up to the 17thC.

A leap forward in design and manufacture occurred at the end of the 18thC, possibly spurred on by the upheaval caused by the French Revolution, which began in 1789. The Compagnie des Cristalleries de Baccarat had been founded in 1765 and began producing lead-crystal glass during the 1780s. Following the end of the Napoleonic Wars in 1815, European markets stabilized;

this fact, allied to a protectionist economic policy in France, helped the Baccarat factory to become one of the major European manufacturers, producing an enormous range of top-quality items and developing distinctive French forms.

Baccarat cut glass often featured ormolu mounts and other gilded decoration. As well as pieces made from high-quality lead metal, it produced sulphides that appeared as silvery-white inclusions, usually in the form of a portrait, inside clear

*A rare French goblet. c1700, 8.5in (21.5cm) high, G*

108

*A 19thC French enamelled opaline glass vase. 26.25in (66.5cm) high, D*

All the main 19thC French glassworks made glass containing coloured canes. A decorative technique producing a mosaic effect, this was a refinement of earlier Venetian styles. The best-known examples of this form of decoration are seen in paperweights made by Baccarat, St. Louis and another famous factory, Clichy. These

and coloured glass. Enamelled crests were used in a similar way and were also very popular. Another characteristic Baccarat product was *verre opaline* – white or pastel-coloured opaque glass. These pieces were usually beautifully shaped and made in a Classical style. Another well-known factory, the Saint-Louis Glassworks, was also founded in the mid-18thC, and produced lead crystal from around the same time as Baccarat, but its styles were less influenced by its mainly Irish workers, and its wares were more distinctive from an earlier date.

*A late 19thC French gilt-bronze and cut-glass centrepiece. 17.5in (44.5cm) high, D*

factories made a huge range in many different colours and styles, and are all extremely high quality. Made principally during the 1840s and 1850s, they are highly collectable, appear regularly at auction and represent some of the most important French glass ever made.

# Baccarat

*A Baccarat cameo glass vase, exhibited at the 1867 Paris Exhibition. 24in (61cm) high, A*

1. Is the glass high-quality lead crystal?
2. Is the cutting skilfully executed?
3. Does the piece appear unusually large?
4. Is it a particularly "French" style?
5. Does the piece have gilding, or gilt highlights?
6. Does it have gilt or ormolu mounts (silver is very rare)?
7. If there is a mark, does it appear on the mount rather than on the glass itself?

# Baccarat (1765–present)

Baccarat, a town in north-eastern France, is the site of the Compagnie des Cristalleries de Baccarat, founded in 1765. Production of cut lead crystal (based on British techniques and using Irish expertise) began in the 19thC. With Val Saint Lambert and Saint-Louis, it made some of the earliest and best mechanically-pressed glass in Europe. Known also for its paperweights, it remains a leading manufacturer.

*A pair of Baccarat Art Nouveau crystal vases. 7.25in (18.5cm) high, F*

*A late 19thC Baccarat cranberry glass punchbowl. 9in (23cm) high, E*

The delicate shade of pink seen on this punchbowl above is a distinctive feature of many Baccarat wares. The characteristic gilt and etched decoration and gilt-metal-mounted foot are also present. Classical decoration was also popular.

## Marks

• Baccarat wares made from pressed glass, and those with ormolu mounts made before the end of the 19thC, are marked with the name "Baccarat".

• Items with paper labels were made around 1900.

• Pieces with acid-stamped marks are almost all 20thC.

• An impressed butterfly is found on Baccarat glassware from the 1920s and 1930s.

• Anything marked "France" is modern.

## Other Baccarat wares

Pieces made from opaline glass form another distinctive group of wares. Baccarat rock crystal-style wares are characterized by their delicate form and heavy weight. Baccarat first exhibited rock crystal engraving at the Paris Exhibition of 1878.

# Saint-Louis

**Saint-Louis (1867–present)**
The glassworks at Saint-Louis, Lorraine, produced clear crystal tablewares from 1781, often with "paperweight" or coloured cane decoration on the bottle stoppers. Glasses and vases may have *millefiori* (Italian for "a thousand flowers") decoration, a term used to describe the mosaic glass found in paperweights, and these are invariably Saint-Louis (see pp 134–5). The factory still produces similar items, but 20thC pieces are distinguished by a mark on the base. Another typical form of decoration is *latticinio*, as seen on the vase below.

*A Saint-Louis turquoise opaline vase. c1850–60, 10in (25.5cm) high, F*

The clear glass body is generally worked with white canes. The top of these pieces may be finished with a cane of the same or a contrasting colour – the usual colours are pink or blue. Examples with internal *latticinio* decoration have a polished out pontil; this distinguishes them from Venetian wares.

**Identification**
• Because they are made from crystal, Saint-Louis pieces are relatively heavy.
• Saint-Louis made most tableware styles, but much of it is difficult to distinguish from that of other manufacturers. Most are valued for their beauty and quality, and not because they can be identified.

*A late 19thC Saint-Louis latticinio presentation vase. 10.5in (26.5cm) high, G*

# Clichy

## Clichy (1837–85)

One of the three great French glassworks, best known today for its paperweights. It was founded in 1837 by Joseph Maès at Billancourt, then had moved to Clichy-la-Garenne, a Paris suburb by 1846.

*A Clichy yellow opaline glass vase, with red and white spiral cable torsade. c1850–60, 5.5in (14cm) high, F*

overlay pieces – and exhibited at international trade fairs in the 1850s and 1860s.

While being more famous for its paperweights (see pp134–5), Clichy also made *latticinio* items. They are usually less flamboyant than pieces by Saint-Louis (see opposite).

The factory's reputation for colour, paperweights and other smaller decorative objects allowed it to prosper throughout the Depression of 1848. At the 1849 Exposition, it showed non-leaded glass that was lighter and clearer than other companies' glass.

The high point was at the Great Exhibition in London in 1851. There it showed glass in shades of blue, red, gold, yellow and black, as well as filigree and *millefiori* pieces. Despite this success, by the end of the 1850s hardly any paperweights were being made and in 1885 it closed down.

*A large mid-19thC Clichy* latticinio *amphora vase, on a metal stand. 15in (38cm) high, F*

## Wares

The factory became well known when it exhibited its coloured and overlaid glass at the French Exposition of Industrial Products in 1844. It went on to produce inexpensive glass for export – mostly coloured and

# Gallé

*A rare marquetry glass crocus vase. c1900, 8.25in (21cm) high, C*

1. Is the piece marked?
2. If marked, is there a star after the name denoting a piece created after Gallé's death?
3. If marked, does it say "Gallé Tip" (meaning "Gallé Style")? These are later copies made in Eastern Europe. NB the "Tip" may not be next to the mark – look carefully!
4. Is it genuine? Fakes are a problem in this market. Look for signs of wear on foot, weight and general quality. Genuine Gallé is well finished, often featuring wheel engraving.

# Galbé (1873–1936)

Emile Gallé (1846–1904) was both a pioneer of the art glass movement and of the Art Nouveau style. Born in the French town of Nancy in 1846 to a family in the glass industry, it was almost inevitable that he should follow in his father's footsteps. He studied botany, chemistry, philosophy and art, followed by learning the techniques of glassmaking at Meisenthal before joining his father at the factory in 1867. By 1873 Gallé had started his own studio and by 1877 he was running the business.

*A late 19thC enamelled pale amber vase, signed "E. Gallé Deposé". 7.5in (19cm) high, G*

Gallé's earliest glass productions are usually clear or transparent glass with gilded and enamelled decoration, often inspired by Japanese art.

After seeing English cameo glass at the 1878 Paris Exhibition, Gallé turned his attention to this art form and began to produce the opaque cameo glass with which we most associate his name.

## Art Nouveau glass

Gallé's newly emerging "Art Nouveau" style made its breakthrough at the 1889 Paris Exhibition to great acclaim, and by 1894 a new factory was built to cope with demand. Gallé continued to experiment and innovate, making use of metallic foils, bubbles and oxides mixed with oils, as well as "inlaying" shaped glass forms into the hot vessels to create his patented technique, Marqueterie-Sur-Verre.

Gallé died in 1904, but his widow, and then son-in-law, continued creating glass until 1936.

*A late 19thC enamel vase, with a translucent brown ribbed glass. 4.25in (11cm) high, G*

*A cameo blown-out vase, signed in design "Gallé". c1900, 10in (25.5cm) high, C*

### Enamelling

Gallé's earliest glass was decorated by means of enamelling and gilding. Designs are often naturalistic or medievalist on traditional shapes. They are almost always transparent glass, which is clear or tinted in soft colours such as a golden honey or "Clair de lune", a pale sapphire.

### Cameo

This is the technique most associated with Gallé. Two or more layers of glass, often with the darkest colour on the outside, are cut by a combination of techniques. Gallé's very best work involves three techniques:

hydrofluoric acid-etching, then mechanical cutting, followed by hand-detailing. Later pieces (known as "Gallé Industriel") were mainly created by acid-etching. Many of these "Industriel" pieces were made after Gallé's death.

### Mould-blown

This technique is also known as "blow out" and "soufflé", and describes pieces that are formed by blowing glass into a mould, often with a design in relief. Although the technique was used in the 1890s, much of the mould-blown work found today dates from the 1920s. High-relief decoration, such as fruits that bulge out from the body, are often polished, giving a contrast to the matt, acid-treated

*A large Lake Como vase, signed within the design "Gallé". c1900, 13.75in (35cm) high, B*

surface. Hand-finishing gives detail to the design, and the hollow raised work adds light and lustre to the finished piece.

**Etude**

Gallé used many complicated techniques, which often pushed the glass to, and sometimes over, the point of destruction. These complex works, which were damaged in some, perhaps minor, way but considered sufficiently worthy of sale, were marked on the base with the word "Etude", meaning "Study".

**Marqueterie-Sur-Verre**

This was a patented technique and perhaps Gallé's greatest expression of glass art. Each piece is an individual work of art where pre-shaped pieces of glass were pushed into a molten blob of glass, rolled smooth and then shaped. It was technically difficult as all the glass sections had to expand and contract at the same rate as they were heated. Once annealed these pieces were usually hand-finished. Many of these pieces are marked "Etude", due to the complex method of manufacture.

**Vase Parlant**

Emile Gallé often referred to his work as "poems in glass" and his "Vase Parlant" or "Talking Vases"

are perhaps the best expression of this. These vases include text, often poetic, as part of the design.

**Cabochons**

This refers to small blobs of moulded or shaped glass, which were applied to the surface of an object to give it a

*An early 20thC cameo glass lamp, signed in design "Gallé". 13.75in (35cm) high, E*

three-dimensional effect, often used as the centre of a flower or sprays of flowers. The glass can be coloured or clear. Clear glass is sometimes laid over metallic foils.

117

# Daum Frères

*An early 20thC Daum etched and enamelled vase, marked "Daum Nancy" with the Cross of Lorraine in gilt. 10in (25.5cm) high, B*

1. Is the piece marked? Daum's products are usually marked and may include "Daum, Nancy" and the Cross of Lorraine.

2. Is the piece damaged or has damage been ground off? Look for differences in colour, where, for example, a foot rim has been ground, exposing the base colour.

3. Is there a polished pontil? Genuine pieces are handmade and will have a polished pontil.

4. Is it good quality? Daum pieces show a subtlety in colouring that reproduction pieces often lack.

## Daum Frères (1878–present)

The Daum family entered the glass business by chance. Jean Daum (1825–85), who had lent money to the proprietors of a glass factory – the Verrerie Sainte Catherine – in Nancy, took over the works when the debt could not be paid. He renamed the factory Verrerie de Nancy. His sons Jean-Louis Auguste (1853–1909) and Jean-Antonin (1864–1931) took over the business in 1885 and renamed it Daum Frères. Jean-Antonin became head of the design studio. Decoration was inspired by the landscape and countryside around Nancy.

*An early 20thC Daum etched and enamelled vase, decorated with gilt violets. 9.5in (24cm) high, D*

*An early 20thC Daum etched and enamelled scenic perfume bottle, signed "Daum Nancy" with Majorelle retail label. 7.75in (19.5cm) high, D*

### Early wares

Early products consisted mainly of table glass, which was exhibited at the 1889 Paris Exhibition. At that exhibition, Emile Gallé (see pp114–17), exhibited the art glass that was to influence Daum's future glass designs. Daum launched its own art glass range in 1891, using cameo glass in the Art Nouveau style. Following Gallé's death in 1904, Daum's innovative designs took centre stage (see pp120–21).

### Art Deco wares

In 1909, Jean-Louis Auguste Daum's son Paul (1888–1944) introduced the Art Deco style to the factory (see pp120–21). It became renowned for its etched, geometric glass and lamps. The glassworks became a public company in 1962 and was renamed Cristallerie Daum.

# Daum Frères wares

## Powdered and applied enamels

Daum introduced a number of decorative techniques. These include *intercalair*, where a powdered glass design is sealed between two layers of glass; and *vitrification des poudres*, a similar technique where designs were created by rolling the hot glass onto a design in powdered glass, then polishing the finished piece until smooth. These were often combined with a *martelé* (hammered metal effect) or frosted background, cameo glass and applied foil-backed decoration to create complex designs such as this rain scene lamp (right). On this example, the trees are set against a frosted background and cameo-carved rain drops extend diagonally around the shade and base to give the effect of

*An early 20thC rain scene lamp, cameo and enamel glass, signed "Daum Nancy". 13in (33cm) high, B*

*A wrought-iron table lamp, by Edgar Brandt and Daum. c1925, 8in (20.5cm) diam, B*

being blown by the wind; the bottom of the shade and base are decorated with green enamel to depict grass and background trees.

## Wrought iron

Before the First World War, Daum worked with metalworkers Edgar Brandt and Louis Majorelle to create simple glass vases and lamps set within intricate, stylized metal mounts. This continued in the 1920s and 1930s.

*A 1930s Art Deco vase, cased with pale celadon enamel. 12.5in (32cm) high, E*

*An Art Deco Joe Descomps for Daum snail pâte-de-verre vide poche. 9.5in (24cm) wide, C*

## Pâte-de-verre

Daum was among the factories that re-introduced the ancient *pâte-de-verre* glass-moulding technique (see p130), using it from 1906–14. It employed the designers Joe Descomps (1869–1950), Amalric Walter (1870–1959) and Henri Bergé (1868–1936) to create small, decorative one-off pieces such as dishes and paperweights featuring small animals, insects and lizards.

*An Art Deco lamp, by A. Daum, shade and base signed. c1925, 18in (46cm) high, C*

## Acid-etched

After the First World War, Daum concentrated on acid-etched decoration, rather than the cameo glass that had made its name during the Art Nouveau period. The factory made vases and lamps in pale, smoky grey or yellow glass with bands of geometric patterns. Some examples

*An Art Deco vase, by Daum, Nancy, with cut geometric decoration. c1925, 5.75in (14.5cm) G*

feature two layers of colour and a variation of the cameo technique. The most desirable to collectors feature deep colours and deep-cut decoration. These new wares were shown at the 1925 Paris Exhibition. In the 1920s Daum also made vases in mottled glass with internal metal foil decoration. These are lighter than the factory's other Art Deco wares (some of which may be too heavy to lift). These pieces are similar in quality to those of Schneider (see p132).

# Other cameo glass

By 1900 French glass factories had overtaken their British rivals as the producers of the best cameo glass. While Gallé and Daum both produced high-end masterpieces, they also began to use acid-etching to cut production time and save money. Many glassworks followed this trend.

*An Arsall cameo glass vase. c1920, 10in (25.5cm) high, G*

## Arsall (late 19thC–1995)

Arsall glass was produced by the Vereinigte Lausitzer Glaswerke, in Weisswasser, Germany, from 1918–38. Floral, acid-etched designs were made between 1918 and 1929. Pieces are signed "Arsall" or "Arsale".

## Burgun, Schverer & Cie (1711-1969)

The Burgun, Schverer & Cie factory was founded in 1711 in the Alsace-Lorraine

*A Burgun, Schverer cameo glass vase, decorated with orchids. 12in (30.5cm) high, C*

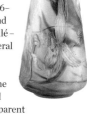

region of France. From 1885–96, designer Désiré Christian (1846–1907) – who had worked for Gallé – developed several techniques: designs were painted onto the glass and cased with transparent glass, which was wheel cut for a three-dimensional effect. Many pieces were finished with a textured *martelé* surface and gilt highlights.

## D'Argental (1919-1925)

The "D'Argental" mark was used by the Compagnie des Cristalleries de Saint-Louis (see p112) on acid-cut cameo glass designed by Paul Nicolas (1875–1952).

*A D'Argental cameo glass vase, by Paul Nicolas. c1925, 7.5in (19cm) high, G*

*A Legras scenic cameo vase. c1920, 7.5in (19cm) high, F*

## Legras & Cie (1895-1936)

The Paris-based Legras glassworks made a successful range of cameo glass inspired by the designs of Gallé and Daum. It produced its first cameo designs in 1900 and won the Grand Prix at the Paris Universal Exposition in the same year. It employed more than 1,000 glassworkers and 150 decorators.

### Müller Frères

Müller Frères was one of the leading French makers of cameo glass. It made high-quality vases and lampshades decorated with landscapes. The

*A Müller Frères cameo scenic table lamp. c1920, 25.5in (65cm) high, E*

glassworks was founded in 1895 at Lunéville, near Nancy, by Henri Müller, who had worked for Gallé. He was later joined by his four brothers and a sister. It made commercial glass and Art Deco lamps until 1933, but closed in 1936.

## Le Verre Français (1918-1933)

Cameo glass marked "Le Verre Français" was produced by the Schneider factory in Epinay-sur-Seine near Paris from 1918 into the 1930s.

The company was founded by brothers Ernest (1877–1937) and Charles (1881–1953) Schneider in 1913. They had both worked

*A Le Verre Français footed vase. c1925, 12.75in (32.5cm) high, E*

for Daum and pieces from their factory resemble those made there. Charles Schneider was a talented designer but art glass by him is rare. Production pieces, many made for export to the USA, are common and feature bright yellow, orange and deep red glass.

# Lalique

*A Lalique "Escargot" deep red glass vase, with moulded
"R.LALIQUE" mark. c1920, 8.25in (21cm) high, C*

1. Is the piece marked? Engraved marks are usually found on the
   base, but moulded marks may be inside a bowl. On complex
   designs they can be hard to find.
2. Is it Lalique? Many firms copied the style; check for known shapes.
3. Is it damaged? Damage reduces the value of Lalique greatly. Check
   that chips have not been ground off. Look for areas that are clear
   which should be matt.
4. If numbered, does it match a known Lalique pattern?

# René Lalique (1860–1945)

René Lalique is today remembered for his glass designs, but he began his career as a jewellery designer. His first glassworks was at Combs-la-Ville, which he rented in 1908–9 and eventually purchased in 1913. By 1919 work had commenced on a new factory at Wingen-sur-Moder in the Alsace region of France, from where the company still operates.

*A Lalique "Rinceaux" lamp, shade with signature "R Lalique France". c1926, 28in (72cm) high, D*

## Wares

The Lalique glassworks produced glass screens, lamps, car mascots, fountains and lights. They were usually worked with frosted white, opalescent glass and rarely used colour. Lalique used naturalistic motifs for decoration, including fish, animals, flowers, leaves and fruit. Generally, Lalique glass is press-moulded with a matt or opalescent appearance, sometimes with a coloured stain. Coloured glass pieces are rare. Rarer still are his *cire perdu*

pieces, which command huge prices (see p126).

## Perfume bottles

Some of his earliest designs were for perfume bottles, often in collaboration with François Coty. Coty approached Lalique to design labels for his creations, but Lalique accepted with the condition that he could design the bottles too.

## Marks

Lalique glass is almost always marked "R. Lalique France". This can be wheel cut, engraved or moulded. After his death, René Lalique's son Marc continued the business as Cristal Lalique, and modern pieces, for example those after 1945, are marked "Lalique, France".

*A Lalique "Poissons" vase, with sepia patina. c1921, 9.5in (24cm) high, D*

# Lalique wares

**Cire perdue**

Technically challenging and inherently rare, *cire perdue* (lost wax) casts are the most eagerly sought of the Lalique glass output. A model for the design was made in wax and this was encased in clay or plaster to create a mould. This was heated to allow the wax to melt and flow out of the mould. Molten glass was then poured into the mould.

*A "Suzanne" statue, with moulded "R. LALIQUE" mark. c1925, 9in (23cm) high, C*

*A "Deux Figures Femmes Aillees" vase, "R. Lalique" mark. 1922, 6.25in (16cm) high, AAA*

The vase above was particularly desirable for its subject matter – two winged female nudes with outstretched arms.

Records in the Lalique catalogue raisonné, compiled by Felix Marcilhac, suggest this vase was created on 13 November 1922, with three other vessels made before 20 November. The design was previously known only from a line drawing and the vase shown here is the only one to emerge on the market.

**Figures and car mascots**

The model of "Suzanne" (above), sometimes called "Suzanne au bain", is one of Laliques most iconic figures. This figure is seen in frosted, white opalescent, amber opalescent or white/blue

*A "Falcon" car mascot, traces of grey staining, with moulded "R. Lalique" mark. c1930, 6.25in (16cm) high, F*

opalescent glass and can be found with an illuminated metal base. Lalique's Art Deco figures are highly sought after. He is considered the "king of the car mascot", with prices for his mascots rising considerably in recent years. The majority are

*A "Deux Figurines" clock, with illuminated metal base. 1926, 15.25in (39cm) high, E*

figural or in the form of animals, posed to suggest speed, power or strength. Many copies were made in France, England and Czechoslovakia, so consider the detailing and size and examine the base for correct marks.

*A "Bacchantes" vase, in opalescent glass with bluish patina and original bronze base, wheel-cut "R. LALIQUE FRANCE". c1927, 9.5in (24cm) high, B*

## Fakes

The success of the Lalique market sadly means that fakes abound. Sometimes genuine glass by other makers have had Lalique marks added, or new glass has been made from Lalique originals. Lalique

*A 1930s Czechoslovakian clear glass "Bacchantes" pattern art glass vase. I*

is highly finished; beware of prominent mould lines and compare to known designs in the Lalique pattern book. The "Bacchantes" vase (left) was often used as inspiration for other factories' designs (see above). Copies may be in a size or type of glass not used by the Lalique factory.

# Sabino

**Mario Ernest Sabino (1878–1961)**
Mario Ernest Sabino was a naturalized Frenchman of Italian origin. From c1920 onwards he produced moulded glass that was very similar to that made by Lalique. His father was a wood carver, and the family moved to Paris while Sabino was a child. He studied at the L'Ecole Nationale des Arts Décoratifs and the Beaux Arts de Paris.

*A 1920s moulded opalescent leaf vase, signed "Sabino, France". 3.75in (9.5cm) high, I*

*A 1920s pink "Danse de Lumière" lamp, with moulded wording. 11.5in (29cm) high, F*

**Wares**
Following the First World War, Sabino saw the potential of the growth of electricity for lighting and established a factory making electric lamps, before moving into glass production. He began to experiment with glass, and by 1925 he had created his own chemical formula for opalescent glass, which looks white or tinted blue in low light but yellow in direct light. Other colours used by the factory included pink and purple. Production stopped during the Second World War, but resumed in 1960, using the original moulds. These later Sabino pieces tend to be slightly different in colour. In 1978 Sabino was sold to the company's American agent, who formed the Sabino Crystal Company, which continues today.

**Marks**
Pieces tend to be marked "Sabino, France" on export pieces and "Sabino, Paris" on domestic products.

# Etling

**La Société Anonyme Edmond Etling & Cie (1919–39)**
Etling is a name often seen on high-quality glass from the 1920s and

*An opalescent bowl. c1920–30, 9in (23cm) diam, H*

1930s. La Société Anonyme Edmond Etling was founded by Parisian retailer Edmond Laurent Etling. He commissioned glass as well as ceramics, ivory and bronze objects, which were sold from his shop at 29 Rue de Paradis. Glass was made at the nearby Choisy-le-Roi glassworks.

**Wares**
Much of Etling's glass was opalescent or frosted, but clear glass was made too, which often has a grey tone. Etling commissioned the top

freelance designers of the day including Lucille Sevin and Geneviève Granger, who designed figural vases with nude females, in their own individual style. The Hungarian sculptor Geza Hiecz designed animals and birds for Etling, while Georges Beal's name is associated with a number of vases with plant designs. Some Etling designs were reproduced by Sèvres Glass in the 1970s, in particular the female nude figurines, which were produced in frosted glass (the originals were opalescent). The shop did not survive the Second World War.

**Marks**
Pieces tend to be marked "Etling", followed by a number.

*A 1920s green vase, moulded in high relief with roses, moulded marks. 9.5in (24cm) high, I*

# Gabriel Argy-Rousseau

**Pâte-de-verre**

First used in ancient times, *pâte-de-verre* was a method of casting powdered glass in moulds, which were then fired in a kiln to melt the glass to shape it. It was rediscovered principally by Frenchman Henri Cros (1840–1907) around 1884. He began to exhibit at the Paris Salons where his work was admired by the director of l'Ecole des Beaux-Arts who found him a kiln to continue his work.

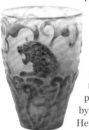

*A "Lions" pâte-de-verre vase, impressed "G. Argy-Rousseau". 1926, 8.75in (22cm) high, C*

**Joseph-Gabriel Argy-Rousseau (1885–1953)**

Joseph-Gabriel Argy-Rousseau initially worked as a ceramicist. In 1921 he established the Société Anonyme des Pâtes-de-Verre d'Argy-Rousseau with gallery and glassworks owner Gustave Moser-Millot.

**Wares**

The firm built new workshops and furnaces and produced a successful range of small, richly coloured Art Nouveau- and Art Deco-style *pâte-de-verre* and *pâte-de-cristal* designs. Decoration included flowers, insects, animals and the female form. The glass ranges in thickness and from semi-transparent to opaque, depending on the design. Pieces are usually signed "G. Argy-Rousseau". The collaboration ended in 1931 following the financial crash of 1929. Argy-Rousseau continued up to the Second World War with limited success.

*An Art Deco Argy-Rousseau pâte-de-verre "Scarabees" vase, signed. 6in (15.5cm) high, C*

# Amalric Walter

**Victor Amalric Walter (1870–1959)**

Amalric Walter's family had a long association with the Sèvres porcelain factory in Sèvres, France. He studied at its school and then worked as a decorator there. Inspired by the work of Henri Cros (see p130), he experimented with the *pâte-de-verre* technique with one of his former tutors Gabriel Lévy.

*A 1920s pâte-de-verre cigarette box, with moulded marks. 9in (23cm) wide, D*

*A pâte-de-verre inkwell, signed "A WALTER NANCY BERGE SC". c1920, 4.25in (11cm) wide, D*

**Wares for Daum**

Walter and Lévy exhibited joint works at the Paris Salon in 1903, which brought them to the attention of Antonin Daum, who offered them a workshop at his eponymous glass works in Nancy (see pp118–21). After a disagreement with Daum, Lévy left, but Walter continued. The pieces produced under Daum were not signed Amalric Walter, but "Daum Nancy". Some pieces were designed by Henri Bergé.

**Later wares**

Following the First World War, Walter established a workshop of his own, marking his wares "A. Walter Nancy" and selling through a network of high-end shops.

Like Argy-Rousseau, Walter found that after 1929 expensive *pâte-de-verre* pieces were losing favour with the public. As a result he introduced cheaper lines, more in tune with the Art Deco style. Between 1935 and 1940 he produced little and began to lose his sight. By the end of the Second World War he was blind, but continued to work until his death, aided by an assistant.

# Blown, cased and enamelled glass

### Mould-blown and cased glass

At the beginning of the 20thC French glassmakers who had already mastered the art of cameo glass turned their attention to blown and cased coloured glass. They used it to create pieces in the Art Deco style with a range of unusual finishes.

*An iridescent blown glass vase, by Maurice Marinot. 1910–20, 11in (28cm) high, E*

### Maurice Marinot (1882–1960)

Painter Maurice Marinot was inspired to work with glass after visiting the Bar-sur-Seine glassworks, which was owned by his friends Eugène and Gabriel Viard.

*A 1920s large Schneider comport. 14in (35.5cm) high, F*

As well as designing glass items, he learnt how to blow it and used his artistic training to create colourful textured pieces, including some with acid-etched decoration.

*A Maurice Marinot bottle, with enamelling around the rim. 1910–20, 6.5in (16.5cm) high, C*

### Schneider and other factories

As well as cameo glass, the Schneider factory (see p123) produced cased glass. Common features such as wrought-iron bases and mottled glass can be seen on this comport. The base features stylized fruit and foliage, and the comport has a black and white striped column and a shallow circular bowl cased in clear crystal. Other factories that produced cased glass included Daum Frères (see pp118–21) and Baccarat (see p110).

*A Jean Luce vase, decorated with flower stems and stripes. c1928, 5.25in (13cm) high, I*

## Enamelled glass

In Europe, there has been a tradition of enamelled decoration on glass since the 15thC. In the 1920s, freehand painting with coloured enamels was being used for both art glass and affordable tablewares. Enamelling cannot be repaired and so any damage will be reflected in the price.

### Jean Luce (1895–1959)

Paris-based Jean Luce began his career designing ceramics, but

*A 1920s Legras enamelled glass vase, decorated with a floral roundel. 18in (46cm) high, F*

soon added glass to his portfolio. He used stylized naturalistic and geometric motifs. He created designs for Cristalleries de Saint-Louis among others.

### Marcel Goupy (1886–1954)

From 1818, designer Marcel Goupy created table and decorative wares painted with simple, enamelled decoration of stylized figural and floral designs. Some pieces are decorated on the inside and the outside to create complex and sophisticated shading to the motifs. Most pieces carry an enamelled "M. Goupy" signature.

*A Marcel Goupy enamelled vase, with gilt highlights. c1930, 7in (18cm) high, E*

### Legras & Cie (1864–present)

The mottled glass used for Legras' cameo designs (see p123) was also used as a base for hand-painted enamel designs. Many of these feature flowers or landscapes. Most pieces are signed "Legras".

133

# Paperweights

## Paperweights

The best paperweights were made by the three French manufacturers, Baccarat (see pp110–11), Saint-Louis (see p112) and Clichy (see p113), during the 1840s. In the 1850s some French glassmakers emigrated to the United States, and important weights were made by the New England Glass Co. (see p221), Boston & Sandwich Glass Co. (see pp186–87), and Mount Washington Glass Co. (see pp184–85). George Bacchus & Sons, Birmingham, and Paul Ysart, Caithness, (see p104) made good British paperweights.

*A Baccarat paperweight, with an upset muslin ground. c1850, 3in (7.5cm) diam, E*

## Technique

Paperweights are made using small sections of coloured glass rods or "canes", placed in a mould, and set in clear glass. The arrangements used by each maker help to identify them.

## Baccarat

Baccarat produced paperweights c1845–9. Many were made from clear crystal with canes cut to resemble tiny flowers. The densely packed stylized decoration, known as *millefiori* (Italian for "thousand flowers") sometimes appeared with silhouettes. The silhouettes on the weight shown left include a reindeer,

*A Baccarat* millefiori *paperweight with 1848 date cane. 3in (7.5cm) diam, D*

elephant, dog and butterfly. The all-over ground shown above is known as "muslin". Sometimes a "signature cane" appears; these give the date the weight was made and include 1846, 1847, 1848 and 1849.

• Others were made from clear and coloured glass set with silvery-white sulphide pictorial medallions.

**Saint-Louis**

Saint-Louis produced paperweights 1844–50. A few are marked with dates between 1845 and 1849, but the most usual date is 1848.

Many Saint-Louis weights were made with a *latticinio* ground (threads of glass arranged in a lattice design), usually in white or pink. They tend to have higher domes than Baccarat, and usually have star-cut bases.

*A Saint-Louis Dahlia paperweight, with star-cut base. c1850, 3in (7.5cm) diam, C*

*A Clichy paperweight, with six circlets of millefiori canes. c1850, 3in (7.5cm) diam, D*

**Clichy**

The best Clichy weights, produced 1846–52, are never dated, and when signed rarely feature anything other than a "C" within the pattern.

• Other forms of decoration favoured by Clichy include coloured swirls, and flower weights incorporating a small rose-shaped cane that came to be known as the "Clichy rose".

• Weights are often spherical, with a flat, slightly concave base.

• Clichy weights are judged to be the best and tend to be expensive.

**Collecting**

Size is important: most weights measure 2–4in (5–10cm) in diameter; unusual sizes, including miniature weights, with a diameter of less than 2in (5cm), are sought after.

# Low Countries and Central European glass

Central Europe (an area that now comprises of Germany, Austria, Hungary, Poland and Czechoslovakia) imported all glass supplies from Rome in the 2ndC and 3rdC. By the 12thC, however, a domestic industry had been established based on *waldglas* or "forest glass", a pale green, transparent metal made using ash from ferns and bracken. Distinctive German vessels began to develop, including the *roemer* (a drinking vessel with an ovoid bowl and a hollow stem), the *kuttrolf* (a decanter with a large surface area for cooling spirits) and the *nuppenbecher* (a prunted beaker). A Venetian

*A late 17thC wheel-and diamond-point engraved German pokal. 7in (18cm) high, C*

influence is visible in the style of decoration: most often "prunts", or applied blobs of glass, or trailed decoration.

Glass produced in the Low Countries (including Holland, Belgium and Luxembourg) during the Middle Ages was principally *waldglas* made in traditional German forms. In the 16thC, however, Italian glassworkers settled in Holland and Belgium, and glasshouses began to produce *façon de Venise* glassware.

*Façon de Venise* was also produced at many centres in Germany, including Dresden, Munich and Nuremberg, but medieval German vessels were also made for local markets. German craftsmen became expert at several methods of decoration, including many types of enamelling. One notable innovation was *Schwarzlot*, which involved painting thinly applied, transparent enamels (usually black, but iron red is found) onto a clear glass body. Sometimes gilt highlighting was also added.

Engraving was popular in both central Europe and the Low Countries between the 16thC and 18thC. Diamond-point engraving began in Europe c1560, and wheel engraving was first carried out in Germany, particularly around Bohemia. These techniques spread to the Low Countries where craftsmen produced extremely high-quality work. The further development of wheel engraving was given a boost by the invention of a heavier, more substantial and better-quality metal in around 1700 made from potash (potassium carbonate) mixed with chalk or lime (calcium carbonate), and by the introduction of water-powered cutting wheels. This led to the production of glass cut in high relief, in a rock crystal style. Many goblets and beakers were also engraved elsewhere in central Europe. "Gold sandwich glass" or

*A rare 17thC Dutch façon de Venise goblet. 12.5in (32cm) high, B*

*Zwichengoldglas,* is another notable German decorative form. At the end of the 18thC and beginning of the 19thC, Bohemia became a centre for experimentation with different types of coloured glass. This group includes: Friedrich Egermann's ruby and gold topaz chloride stains and Lithyalin, a coloured, marbled glass made to imitate agate and other semiprecious stones; Josef Reidel's yellow/green uranium glass, known as *Annagelb* and *Annagrün*; and Count von Buquoy's opaque black Hyalith. 19thC German and Bohemian glass was characterized by two fashions: the Biedermeier and Historismus, styles (see pp142–3).

In the 19thC, glasshouses in Holland and Belgium such as Val Saint Lambert and Vonêche produced high-quality wares in a European style. Unfortunately, pieces are not easy to attribute to particular factories.

*An exhibition vase, by Steigerwald of Munich. 1862, 12.75in (32.5cm) high, E*

# Engraved Dutch drinking glasses

*A Dutch engraved light baluster armorial and ship goblet. c1750, 9.75in (25cm) high, D*

1.  Is the engraving shallow and highly skilled?
2.  Are the engraved lines ragged and slightly broken?
3.  Does the decoration feature a Dutch inscription or a Dutch subject?
4.  If signed, is the signature on the foot (signatures found anywhere else are more unusual)?
5.  If stipple engraved, is the subject allegorical, Jacobin or a portrait?
6.  Can the design be seen clearly only at a certain angle?

## Diamond-point engraving

An ancient method of glass decoration, diamond engraving became particularly popular in the Low Countries, c1600–1800. It involves using a diamond- or metal-tipped stylus to scratch a pattern on the surface of the glass. The cutting is not deep and lines are often slightly ragged and broken, in contrast to the hard lines created by wheel engraving. From the mid-17thC a number of tall flute glasses were made in the *façon de Venise* style; most now belong to museum collections although some are offered for sale. They were usually made as commemorative pieces or to special commission.

## Stipple-point engraving

In spite of changing fashions abroad, diamond-point engraving remained popular in the Netherlands. It was gradually refined, and c1780 a technique known as stipple engraving was introduced. Instead of using the diamond stylus to cut lines, it was tapped on the surface to create

*A fine Dutch stipple-engraved "Newcastle" composite stemmed cordial glass. c1760, 7in (18cm) high, D*

designs consisting of minute dots. The density of the dots created the effect of light and shade.

The detail on stipple-engraved glass is often so fine that the design can only be seen clearly when held up to the light at the same angle as the stylus struck the glass. The most famous craftsmen were Frans Greenwood (1680–1761) and David Wolff (1732–98).

Designs include allegorical subjects, portraits and Jacobin motifs supporting the French Revolution.

## Collecting

• On early pieces, minor damage will not significantly affect value.

• A signed piece is worth twice as much as one that is unsigned. Stipple-engraved pieces are more often signed and are valuable.

*A Dutch engraved light baluster goblet. c1750, 7.5in (19cm) high, E*

# Schwarzlot

*A goblet with Schwarzlot paintings from Saxony, Germany. c1730, 8.75in (22cm) high, G*

1. Is the design black, brown and/or red?
2. Is it highly detailed and beautifully executed?
3. Is the glass item itself small and unremarkable?
4. If the piece is a tumbler, does it have three ball feet?
5. If there is a signature, does it belong to an artist rather than a factory?
6. Is the piece gilded?
7. Does the clear body have a soft tone?
8. Is the design painted and not printed onto the glass?

## Early Schwarzlot glass

In the mid-17thC a new decorative technique was developed in Nuremberg by Johann Schaper (1621–70). His method involved freehand painting in a black (*Schwarzlot*) or iron-red (*Eiserot*) enamel wash. The style is known as *Schwarzlot*, and was popular until the mid-18thC. Most early pieces can be attributed to Schaper or his followers: the most important of these were Johann Faber and Abraham Helmack. They decorated low beakers, usually with three feet. The items they decorated were often incidental to the design.

*A Friedrich Egermann decanter. c1840, 14in (35.5cm) high, G*

### Subjects

The most common subjects found on early *Schwarzlot* glass include hunting scenes, tales from mythology, Romantic landscapes, coats of arms and harbour scenes.

## Ignaz Preissler (b.1670)

Together with his father Daniel (1636–1733), Ignaz Preissler developed the production of *Schwarzlot* glass. He used gilt, which added depth and richness. A revival of *Schwarzlot* glass took place towards the end of the 19thC, spurred on by the Historismus movement (see p143). Louis Lobmeyr, a Viennese industrialist and glass designer, was the driving force behind the renewal of production. His factory made very good-quality copies, painted with hunting or German folk and peasant scenes. Other factories tried to produce *Schwarzlot*, but without the same success.

### Beware

Some later copies were transfer-printed rather than painted.

*A Meyr's Neffe cover Cup, with colourless glass decorated in gold and black stain. c1880, 12.5in (32cm) high, E*

141

# Biedermeier glass

*A glass beaker, with a view of Rome, by Gottlob Mohn, Vienna. c1820, 4.5in (11.5cm) high, C*

1. Is the piece a straight-sided or waisted beaker?
2. Is the painted decoration very high quality?
3. Does the design feature a Germanic subject or motif?
4. Is there any gilt detailing?
5. Is the decoration in good condition?
6. If signed, does the signature appear on the base or the reverse of the painting?

## Biedermeier glass

The Biedermeier style characterized a period of middle-class prosperity in Germany following the end of the Napoleonic Wars (c1815–45).

## Samuel and Gottlob Mohn

The masters of the medium were Samuel Mohn (1762–1815) and his son Gottlob (1789–1825). They worked in thinly applied, translucent enamels, most commonly on straight-sided beakers. Subjects included panoramic views (such as the beaker shown opposite), and romantic and allegorical designs. Gottlob moved to Vienna in 1811 and influenced a number of craftsmen.

*A Kothgasser-Ranftbecher glass. c1825, 4.25in (11cm) high, C*

One of the enamellers influenced by the Mohns was Anton Kothgasser (1759–1851). Other famous enamellers included C. von Scheidt, Andreas Mattoni (Karlsbad) and C. F. Hoffmeister (Vienna). Viennese Biedermeier glasses were made as expensive souvenirs, and were given as gifts.

### The Historismus movement

Following the re-establishment of the German Empire in 1871, many traditional forms were reproduced as part of an effort to establish a unified national heritage. This movement was part of a Historismus trend in Europe where old Venetian styles were also being copied. Many German pieces were based on medieval and Renaissance glass of the Tyrol and Bohemia as well as the area around the German-Polish border. Popular forms included *Humpen* (a tall cylindrical beer glass), *Roemer* (15th and 16thC drinking vessel), *Kuttrolf* (a cooling bottle) and *Daumenglas* (a barrel-shaped beaker).

*A late 19thC German Historismus amber glass chalice, with applied prunts and enamel decoration. 12.5in (32cm) high, G*

# 19thC other engraved and decorated glass

*An early 18thC German glass goblet, with cover. 14.5in (37cm) high, F*

1. Is the engraving fluid and sophisticated?
2. Does it feature a Germanic motif – for example, a landscape or woodland scene?
3. Is the design detailed and well drawn?
4. If coloured, does the piece feel relatively heavy?
5. Is the cutting and engraving heavy and ornate?
6. Is the piece signed by the artist?
7. Is the signature hidden within the engraved design?

## 19thC Bohemian engraving

Bohemian engraved glass underwent a change of style during the 19thC. The stiff, formal late 18thC designs became fluid and sophisticated. Engravers in Bohemia were without equal; vases "carved" to imitate rock crystal are some of the finest examples of their skills.

*A pair of late 19thC Moser decanters, with applied decoration. 14.5in (37cm) high, C*

## Subjects

In the 19thC, craftsmen began to work with coloured glass, and vessels with more interesting shapes. This gave them greater scope for their designs, and popular subjects included idealized landscapes, woodland scenes, hunting, horses and battles. The most characteristic form of Bohemian engraving was on overlay or flashed glass bodies. Cased or overlay glass is covered with one or more coloured outer layers.

Flashed glass has a colour stained onto the outside, which is then annealed to make the colour permanent. The coloured layer is engraved to show the glass body underneath. Flashed glass was usually a less expensive substitute for overlay glass.

## J. & L. Lobmeyr

The Lobmeyr factory was founded by Josef Lobmeyr in 1822. Towards the end of the 19thC his sons Louis and Josef Jnr helped to revive past techniques and produced *Schwarzlot*, enamelled and rock crystal-style glass.

Pieces by Lobmeyr were sometimes signed, but the signatures may be hard to find and are often worked into the pattern.

*An engraved ewer and goblet, by J. & L. Lobmeyr. c1880, ewer 9.75in (25cm) high, H*

# 19thC coloured Bohemian glass

*A large 19th C Bohemian glass goblet and cover. 20.25in (51.5cm) high, E*

1. Is the colour rich and solid with a thin outer layer?
2. Is clear glass visible through the engraving?
3. If engraved, does the design feature Germanic motifs (see pp144–5)?
4. Is the glass body heavy and high quality?
5. Is the piece free from chips and other damage?
6. Is the stem free from chips and other damage?
7. Does the glass have an elaborate foot?

## Colouring glass

In the 19thC three main methods were used to colour glass:

• Adding a metal oxide to the batch.

• Casing or overlay, where clear glass is covered with a coloured outer layer.

• Staining or flashing, where clear glass is covered with a thin layer of colour. Staining involves the application of metal oxides to clear glass by painting or dipping the item into the stain. This creates a rich, solid colour. Flashing is a less expensive method and involves applying a thin layer of coloured glass to a clear body.

*A Bohemian uranium glass decanter. c1840, 13in (33cm) high, H*

*A Bohemian lidded cup, with an enamel overlay. c1840, 12.5in (32cm) high, H*

## Bohemian coloured glass

Many different colours for glass, including violet and pink, were developed. The use of ultramarine brought new shades of blue from very pale blue to almost black.

One of the most unusual new colours, discovered by Josef Riedel was a transparent yellow-green (*Annagrün*) and green-yellow (*Annagelb*) glass, produced by adding small quantities of uranium. It was also used to produce an opaque, apple-green glass, known as chrysoprase.

Friedrich Egermann produced a ruby stain and a yellow stain from silver chloride, and an agate-like effect on glass called Lithyalin.

## Collecting

• Flashed items were usually less expensive and tended to be made from lower-quality materials than those that were stained.

• The quality of the colour, and overall condition, are the main determinants of the value.

• Feel the item carefully to detect any damage: often chips are less obvious on coloured glass.

147

# Kralik

## Wilhelm Kralik Sohne (1841–1940s)

Wilhelm Kralik Sohne was one of the largest Bohemian art glass producers in the early 20thC. At its best, this company's products compare to those of Tiffany and Loetz, for whom they are often mistaken. Wilhelm Kralik (1806–77) operated seven glassworks, operating collectively under the name Meyr's Neffe, which he had inherited in 1841. Following Willhelm's death the factory was run by his sons. Two of the former Meyr's Neffe works were amalgamated by Heinrich Kralik (1840–1911) to form Wilhelm Kralik Sohne, a firm that continued until the 1940s.

*A Kralik vase in an Art Nouveau metal frame. c1910, 23in (58.5cm) high, D*

## Wares

Kralik produced a wide range of innovative designs, which can be hard to identify, as they are very similar to work by other makers.

• Its *martelé* (hammered) glass is typical of its output and is often seen with applied flowers or spiral trails called "rigaree" and on a pearlized base.

• Iridescent swirled glass is often

*A Kralik red-banded vase, with pulled rim and heavily iridized surface. c1905, 6in (15cm) high, H*

encountered with Art Nouveau mounts, which may be flat in form.

• It is generally easier to find the more affordable production lines, which were sold in Europe and the USA.

• The art glass is generally harder to identify and locate and can therefore command higher prices.

# Pallme-König

## Pallme-König (1786–1958)

Pallme-König is remembered for its high-quality Art Nouveau art glass, although the origins of the company go back to the late

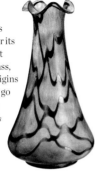

*A vase with trails on an iridescent ground. c1900, 10in (25.5cm) high, H*

18thC. A glassworks was established in 1786 by Ignaz Pallme-König in Steinschönau, which he called Pallme Ullmann. Over a century later his grandsons Joseph and Theodore Pallme-König joined with a glasshouse at Kosten owned by William Habel to form Gebruder Pallme-König & Habel. While similar to that produced by Loetz, its art glass production was never on the same scale.

## Wares

During the Art Nouveau period, Pallme-König employed 300 craftsmen to produce art and table glass. They produced iridescent glass that often features trailing in contrasting colours. These trails were applied to the molten glass before the glass was blown into a mould, which gives them a characteristic flattened appearance. They are often said to look like a spider's web. Similar glass by other makers, such as Loetz, tends to feature thinner trails, which stand more proud. These vases are often worked at the top, by cutting the hot glass and folding it back. However, Pallme-König wares lacked the delicacy, quality and controlled iridescence of wares by firms such as Loetz. This style of glass was in production until the 1920s.

## Marks

Pallme-König wares are generally unmarked and so attribution can be difficult.

*A pair of iridescent glass vases, with amethyst banding. c1900, 8in (20.5cm) high, H*

# WMF

*A 1930s Ikora vase, designed by Karl Wiedmann. 17in (43cm) high, G*

1. Is the glass lightweight, thinly blown and with a thin layer of iridescent film?
2. Is the glass thick, free-blown and cased?
3. If cased, has it been mould-blown or dip-moulded?
4. If otherwise unmarked, are there traces of a paper label?
5. Does the glass feature complex decoration such as silver and copper leaf? Has it been sandblasted or is there a cut design?
6. Does the glass have air bubbles and/or inclusions?

## WMF/Württembergische Metallwarenfabrik (1880–present)

WMF – founded in Geislingen near Stuttgart, Germany, in 1880 – is probably best known for its Art Nouveau metalware, but it made glass from 1883. The original glassworks was destroyed during the First World War. A replacement, modern, factory was built in 1922.

*A "Myra" bulbous vessel-shaped vase, with colourless glass and golden lustre. 1925, 6in (15.5cm) high, G*

*An Ikora vase, clear glass inlaid with dark brown and amber. c1935, 16in (40.5cm) high, G*

### Wares

By 1925 glass technician Karl Wiedmann (1905–92) had developed Myra-Kristall – a range of iridescent glass named after an ancient archaeological site in Asia Minor. A year later, the first pieces of the Ikora-Kristall range of art glass were made.

• Myra-Kristall featured lightweight, thinly blown shapes with a thin layer of iridescent film.

• Ikora-Kristall featured thick, free-blown cased glass, which was mould-blown or dip-moulded. It was made until 1954.

• Ikora featured mass-produced ranges that were generally inexpensive and unmarked, although a few pieces had paper labels.

• The Ikora-Unica series was largely one-off pieces made mostly for exhibition. They featured more complex decoration such as silver and copper leaf, sandblasted or cut patterns. WMF was forced to sell these pieces after the Second World War.

The WMF glassworks was closed in 1982 and glass production was moved overseas.

# Enamelled glass

German and Bohemian glassworks had a strong tradition of decoration glass with enamel designs. Transparent coloured enamels were first used on Biedermeier beakers (see pp142–3), but they came into their own on the Art Nouveau and

*A pair of vases, by Wally Weisenthiel. 1910–20, 8.5in (21.5cm) high, C (pair)*

Art Deco drinking glasses made by factories such as Theresienthal (see below), Moser (see pp154–5), J. & L. Lobmeyer (seep145) and Meyr's Neffe (see p148).
## Wiener Werkstätte
The enamelling on glass technique was also used by members of the Wiener Werkstätte (see p159),

including Wally Weisenthiel (see left), Michael Powolny (see p158) and Josef Hoffmann (see p159). Designs included stylized flowers and landscapes such as hunting scenes.
## Theresienthal Glassworks (1836–present)
The Theresienthal Glassworks specialize in enamelled and very delicate wine glasses and tableware. They are never signed. After 1861, three generations of the von Poschinger family ran the glassworks. In 1897, Michael (1834–1908) handed the factory to his son Benedikt (1864–1915). He in turn handed it to sons Hans (1892–1951) and Egon (1894–1977). The works were taken over by Hutschenreuther AG, Selb, in 1982.

*A Theresienthal wine glass, with enamelled and gilded bowl. c1902, 8.5in (21.5cm) high, H*

# Cameo glass

In the late 19thC and early 20thC glassmakers led the way in the manufacture of cameo glass. However, this did not prevent German and Bohemian factories producing successful, home-grown cameo wares. Some were inspired by masterpieces by Gallé and Daum, creating many layers of cameo glass enhanced by wheel cutting and applied decoration. Others, such as Vallerysthal and Loetz, developed a distinctive, two-colour cameo glass that proved to be an ideal medium for Art Nouveau and Art Deco motifs.

**Harrach Glassworks (1712–present)**
In the 19thC, this factory in Harrachov, Bohemia, was renowned for its luxury tablewares.

*An early 20thC Moser cameo glass vase. 5in (12.5cm) high, H*

*A rare Harrach cameo vase, signed. c1900, 14in (35.5cm) high, F*

But by 1900 it had become a pioneer in Art Nouveau glass and produced glass for companies such as J. & L. Lobmeyr (see p145) and Moser (see above and pp154–5).
As early as 1903, Jan Kotera, Julius Jelinek and Alois Metalek were producing Modernist designs for the Harrach factory.
The Art Nouveau vases on this page are typical of the designs produced in Europe at the beginning of the 20thC. The Harrach vase (left) has a mottled green ground and acid-etched red and purple flowers. A similar technique was used on the Moser vase (above). It has the added detail of a ruffled rim. Both feature naturalistic flowers, which enhance the shape of the glass vessel. Later, Art Deco designs often featured bands of stylized flowers and leaves.

# Ludwig Moser & Sons

*A 20thC vase, with a carved design of a "maiden with a rose"
and gilt band to neck. 9.25in (23.5cm) high, H*

1. Is the decoration engraved or enamelled onto the glass?
2. Is the colourful art glass decorated with bands of gilding and
   etched patterns?
3. Is there cameo decoration of an animal or jungle scene? Has it
   often been highlighted with gold enamel or gilt decoration?
4. Is the cameo design in relief?
5. Is the glass marked with an etched mark or paper label? Marks
   include "Moser", "Moser Karlsbad" (or Carlsbad) and "MM
   Glasfabrik Karlsbad".

## Ludwig Moser & Sons (1857–present)

Austrian-born Ludwig Moser (1833–1916) was an influential painter, book illustrator, and jewellery, glass, textile and furniture designer; he was also an architect.

In 1857 Moser opened a glass workshop in Karlovy Vary, Bohemia. It specialized in polishing, engraving and cutting

*A green and flashed red glass vase, with cut and etched decoration. c1928, 10in (25.5 cm) high, H*

glass. The company began making its own glass in 1893 when, with his sons Gustav and Rudolf, Moser founded a glass factory in Karlsbad that employed 400 people. Within a short time, he gained a reputation as the most prestigious producer of crystal in the Austro-Hungarian Empire. The company made tablewares made from clear glass and decorated with engraved and enamelled designs.

## 20thC wares

Moser's wares changed in 1909 when its designers began to create coloured art glass vases and bowls with bands of gilding and etched patterns.

In the 1920s the factory began a successful collaboration with the Wiener Werkstätte designer Josef Hoffmann (see p159). As well as drinking glasses, Hoffmann created vases with cameo glass animal and jungle scenes. These relief images were often highlighted with gold enamel or gilt decoration.

By 1922 Moser was the largest producer of high-end drinking and decorative glass in Bohemia. Business suffered during the Depression of the 1930s, and the Moser family sold its shares in 1938. The company is now publicly owned.

*A vase with a relief design by Heinrich Hussmann. c1930, 7.5in (19cm) high, G*

155

# Loetz

*A "Phänomen Gre
358" vase, by Josef
Hoffmann. 1900, 7in
(18cm) high, B*

1. Is the vase ovoid, tapered or baluster-shaped? Are there handles?
2. If gourd-shaped, does the vase have an extended neck?
3. Has the glass been pinched or crimped?
4. Is the rim flared or ruffled?
5. Are the colours highlighted with iridescence?
6. Is the pattern a graduation of a solid colour; a stylized or naturalistic plant-form motif; or abstract?
7. Is it engraved on the base with "Loetz/Austria" in script?

## Loetz (1840–1940)

Johann Loetz (1778–1848) founded his factory in 1840, in Klostermühle, Bavaria. From 1848 it was run by his widow as Glasfabrik Johann Loetz-Witwe. It was taken over by Max Ritter von Spaun in 1879. He modernized the production process and introduced new techniques.

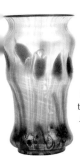

*A rare "Cristall" vase, by Franz Hofstötter. 1900, 10in (25.5cm) high, B*

### Early wares

Early wares included art glass that simulated hardstones, and cameo glass. But it was the iridescent glass developed during the 1890s that captured the public imagination.

### Forms and shapes

Loetz's vases were designed in numerous and diverse shapes:
• Ovoid, tapering or baluster-shaped vases, some with handles.
• Gourd-like vases and those with rose-sprinkler "bird's neck" vases. Details include pinched sides and crimped, flared or ruffled rims.

### Colours and patterns

Typical colour combinations are shades of red, gold and dark honey, deep purple with silver and blue iridescence, and yellow or amber with green-gold iridescence. Patterns include graduations of solid colour, stylized or naturalistic plant-forms, and "abstract" compositions such as "pulled feather", "lava-like", "papillon" (which resembles butterfly wings and is also referred to as "oil-spot"); and "Phanomen" (or Phenomenon).

### Marks

Loetz used various marks. The mostly common is "Loetz/Austria" engraved in script. Forged signatures are known.

*A Josef Hoffmann "Luna" vase in a wooden frame. 1899, 15.5in (39.5cm) high, D*

157

# Michael Powolny

**Michael Powolny (1871–1954)**
Austrian Michael Powolny is best known as a ceramicist, sculptor and one of the founders of the Vienna Secession and Wiener Werkstätte movements. As a teacher

*A corseted vase, with cobalt trailing, designed for Loetz. c1914, 5in (12.5cm) high, F*

– he was made a professor at the Kunstgewerbeschule in Vienna in 1912 – and craftsman, Powolny influenced Austrian, British and US ceramics during the 1930s. In 1906 Powolny set up the Wiener Keramik Studio with graphic artist Berthold Löffler (1874–1960). Powolny's glass designs number about 25; examples of his most popular are vessels with vertical stripes as shown here.

**Glass designs**
The studio employed designers from the new Wiener Werkstätte and Powolny became one of its leading designers. From 1913 he created a small range of stylish glass for the Wiener Werkstätte. Powolny worked with leading Austrian glassworks including J. & L. Lobmeyer (see p145) and Loetz (see pp156–7). Many of these pieces were in the Wiener Werkstätte style: blown-cased forms

*A cased glass vase of classic urn shape, with black stringing. c1914, 7in (18cm) high, I*

with contrasting black linear details. These details highlighted the shapes of the vases and anticipated the Art Deco movement. As a result they continued to sell into the 1930s.

# Josef Hoffmann

**Josef Hoffmann (1870–1956)**
The Austrian architect Josef Hoffmann was a highly influential designer. In 1897 he founded the Vienna Secession, an alliance of artists, designers and architects,

*A footed bowl, made by Meyr's Neffe for the Wiener Werkstätte. 1917, 6in (15.5cm) high, F*

who broke from the Viennese Society of Visual Artists in 1897.
Then, in 1903 he founded the Wiener Werkstätte with Koloman Moser and Fritz Wärndorfer. The organization – an association of craftsmen – employed 100 workers (including 40 "masters") and made furniture, metalwork and glass of progressive design in a range of styles. It aimed to rescue the decorative arts from poor standards of design and workmanship. By 1910 the founders

had been joined by Joseph Olbrich, Gustav Klimt, Dagobert Peche and Otto Prutscher, among others. Only a small, avant-garde and wealthy group of buyers could afford its wares and consequently the Wiener Werkstätte closed in 1932.

**Glass designs**
Hoffmann's glass designs feature the rectilinear style seen in much of his work. Many pieces resemble his metalware – scallop-shaped bowls with trumpet-shaped feet. They were made by factories including Meyr's Neffe and Moser.
He also designed furniture (often for Thonet), metalwork and jewellery.

**Marks**
Glass made for the Wiener Werkstätte may be etched "WW" on the base.

*A scallop-edged bowl, made for the Wiener Werkstätte. c1915, 10in (25.5cm) diam, E*

# Val Saint-Lambert

*A 1930s vase on a clear pedestal foot, cased
blue on the outside and red on the inside.
8in (20.5cm) high, D*

1. Is the transparent cased coloured glass cut on the inside and the
   outside to reveal the colours?
2. Is the glass lead crystal?
3. Is the cut design in a geometric, curved pattern?
4. If the vessel is thick and heavy, are the lines straight and any
   naturalistic motifs abstract?
5. Are the colour contrasts dramatic?
6. Does the mark read "Val St Lambert", "VSL", "Val St Lambert
   Belgique" or "Val St Lambert Déposé"?

# Val Saint-Lambert (1825–present)

The Val Saint-Lambert glasshouse is Belgium's most important glasshouse and was founded in 1825 by François Kemlin and Auguste Lelièvre, at Val Saint-Lambert, just outside Liège.

## Wares

It is best known for its strongly coloured cut glass in the Art Nouveau and Art Deco styles, cut on the inside and outside of the vessel to reveal the colours of the glass.

## Designers

Léon Ledru (1855–1926) was chief designer, 1886–1926. He worked with some of the most important figures in Belgian Art Nouveau, including

*An ovoid vase, cased in dark amethyst over amber glass. c1930, 5.75in (14.5cm) high, E*

*A 1930s vase, in cased red glass cut with vertical bands. The rim has a silver band. 10in (25.5cm) high, F*

Victor Horta (1861–1947) and Henry van de Velde (1863–1957). Van de Velde designed deeply cut patterns that were used on transparent cased coloured vases.

## Art Deco wares

At the 1925 Paris Exhibition the factory exhibited geometric, curved patterns by Ledru and Joseph Simon (1874–1960). These pieces – the Arts Décoratifs de Paris collection – won the Grand Prix. Later Art Deco wares feature straight lines and more abstract naturalistic motifs on thicker, heavier vessels. The colour contrasts also became more dramatic and used on clear and black glass. Simon became chief designer in 1926 and designed transparent cased glass with slashed intaglio patterns. These feature the factory mark and an "S". He was followed by Charles Graffart (1893–1967) from 1929. Graffart created imposing vases with deeply cut, abstract designs.

161

# Scandinavian glass

There is no record of glassmaking in Scandinavia until the mid-16thC. There is archaeological evidence of a primitive glass industry from 1580 to 1650, and written records show that German glassworkers were employed at these factories producing window glass and tablewares. Records also show Venetian glassmakers worked in Stockholm and Copenhagen, but no attributable work exists.

### German influence

By the mid-18thC the Germanic style had become dominant. Two main factories produced this style of wares: Skånska Glasbruket (1691–1808) and Kosta Boda (1742–present). Skånska Glasbruket at Henrikstorp in Scania pioneered the production of Scandinavian cut, coloured glass, especially deep blue and opaque white wares.

*A Scandinavian cream pail, with spiral fluted decoration. c1820, 14.5in (37cm) diameter, H*

### Sweden

In 1686 the Kungsholm Glasbruk was founded by a Muranese glassworker called Giacomo Bernadini Scapitta. It remained active until 1815. It produced some tall, thinly blown *façon de Venise* goblets with unusual stems and decorated with crowns.

*A goblet with nude female figures, designed by Simon Gate. 1926, 18in (46cm) high, E*

Kosta Boda, in Småland, is Sweden's oldest surviving glasshouse and the site of a great deal of more primitive glassmaking. Kosta employed foreign workers throughout the 18thC and 19thC. They made wares that are difficult to distinguish from similar styles produced elsewhere in Europe at the time. Another notable Swedish manufacturer is the Orrefors Glassworks, which was established in Småland in 1898. The company began by producing bottles and tableware, but was increasingly known for its art glass from the 1920s, which was often colourless and engraved with stylized designs. A number of designers worked for the company, including Simon Gate, Edward Hald, Nils Landberg and Vicke Lindstrand.

**Norway and Denmark**

From 1397 to 1814 Norway and Denmark were a single nation with the capital based in Copenhagen. There is no evidence of glassmaking before the founding of a glassworks at Nöstetangen in Drammen, Norway, in 1741, by Caspar Herman von

*An Orrefors vase, cased in brown on black fotklack, engraved by Thure Löfgren, with matt and glossy decor of a dancer. 1934, 7.75in (19.5cm) high, E*

Storm. Originally staffed by German workers, von Storm was quick to respond to changes that were occurring elsewhere in Europe and encouraged two British glassworkers, James Keith and William Brown from Newcastle upon Tyne, England, to work for him. Keith introduced the Anglo-Venetian form to Norway, and some popular 18thC stem forms, including the baluster, air and opaque twist. The glassworks at Nöstetangen produced all forms of glassware, including three chandeliers designed by the Silesian craftsman Heinrich Gottlieb Köhler, who was also famous for his engraving.

**Late 19thC Scandinavian glass**

The late 19thC was a period of change and modernization; many forms were adopted from other areas. Production was high quality, but styles are not distinctive enough to facilitate identification without a signature or mark.

# Orrefors blown glass

*A large glass urn and cover,*
*designed by Simon Gate.*
*c1918, 20in (51cm) high, G*

1. Is the glass clear and colourless or tinted?
2. Is the glass engraved with a stylized design?
3. Does the piece have a simple, sculptural and organic shape?
4. Is the glass of a high quality?
5. Is there any damage? If so the value will be considerably less than a perfect piece.
6. Is the glass marked with a series of letters and numbers?

**Orrefors Glassworks (1898–present)**

The Orrefors factory in Småland, Sweden, is renowned for its art glass. The factory was established in 1898 and began by producing bottles and tablewares, but from the 1920s it was increasingly known for its art glass, which was often colourless and engraved with stylized designs (see pp166–7). Orrefors merged with Kosta Boda in 1990 (see pp168–9).

*A 1930s Art Deco engraved vase, by Edward Hald. 10in (25.5cm) high, I*

**Wares**

There was a long tradition of glassmaking in Sweden, which created a skilled workforce. In the early 20thC these glassmakers worked with a team of talented designers to produce a range of simple sculptural and organic shapes that celebrated the Swedish landscape and the quality of Orrefors glass. As they rely on the perfection of the glass for their appeal any damage is immediately apparent and will affect the value of the piece.

**Designers**

Orrefors designers Simon Gate (1883–1945) and Edward Hald (1883–1980) received acclaim for their wheel-engraved glass at the 1925 Paris Exhibition, where it was referred to as "Swedish Grace". Others celebrated for their engraved glass are Vicke Lindstrand (1904–83) and Sven Palmqvist (1906–84).

**Marks**

All Orrefors glass is marked using a system of letters and numbers. Refer to a specialist guide to decode them.

*A bowl, signed "Orrefors LA355", dated. 1931, 5.25in (13cm) high, I*

# Orrefors engraved and cut glass

*A Graal vase decorated with flowers, designed by Simon Gate and blown*
*by Knut Bergqvist and Heinrich Wollman. 1919, 6.25in (16cm) high, E*

1.  Is a layer of engraved or etched coloured glass held between two
    layers of clear glass?
2.  Is the outer layer a thick layer of clear glass that creates an optical
    effect and make the glass feel heavy?
3.  Is a layer of sandblasted coloured glass held between two layers of
    clear glass?
4.  Are air bubbles trapped inside the glass?
5.  Does the pattern feature an abstract, figurative or animal subject?
6.  Is the glass marked with a series of letters and numbers?

## Orrefors Glassworks (1898–present)

The Orrefors factory in Småland, Sweden, is renowned for its art glass (see pp164–5). In the early 20thC Orrefors' glassblowers and designers developed two new decorative techniques: Graal and Ariel. These helped to put Scandinavian glass at the forefront of 20thC design.

### Graal technique

Graal was first made in 1916. In this complex technique, a layer of engraved or etched coloured glass is held between two layers of clear glass. It was developed by Simon Gate and master glassblower Knut Bergqvist (1873–1953). After 1930, a thick layer of clear glass was added to create an optical effect and a heavy weight.

*An Ariel vase with the profile of a girl, by Edvin Ohrström. 1938, 6.25in (16cm) high, C*

### Ariel technique

The first pieces of Ariel date from 1937. The method was developed by Edvin Ohrström (1906–94), Gustav Bergqvist and Vicke Lindstrand. Again, a layer of coloured glass is held between two layers of clear glass. But in this case the decoration

*A Graal vase, decorated with fish, by Edward Hald. 1944, 7.25in (18.5 cm) high, G*

is sandblasted into the coloured glass, creating channels or holes that trap air when the outer later of glass is applied. These bubbles form part of the design which usually features patterns of abstract, figurative or animal subjects.

The company's reputation for such innovative processes continued with the Ravenna, Kraka and Fuga ranges.

# Kosta Boda

*A 1930s dark green footed vase, with ball knop, designed by Elis Bergh. c1934, 13.75in (35cm) high, I*

1. Is the clear glass pressed or decorated with cutting?
2. Does the piece have a simple shape with an engraved design or internal ribs that are Art Deco in style?
3. Is the decoration Art Nouveau – perhaps cameo – in style?
4. Is the base marked with a date code or signature?
5. Is any wear consistent with decades of use or display on a shelf?
6. Is there any damage (this may be expensive to repair)?

## Kosta Boda (1742–present)

Kosta Boda, in Småland, is Sweden's oldest surviving glass factory. During the 18thC and 19thC it relied on foreign workers to produce its range of window glass, chandeliers and drinking glasses. In the 1840s the factory began to follow the latest trends and technical developments, producing pressed glass from the 1840s, and setting up a new glass-cutting workshop in the 1880s. When it exhibited at the General Art and Industrial Exposition of Stockholm in 1897, it was criticized because its glassware was similar to styles from elsewhere in Europe. As a result, the factory began to employ its own designers, and decorative wares such as Art Nouveau cameo glass were produced.

*A 1930s vase, engraved with a mermaid, by Lars Kjellander. 6.5in (16.5cm) high, H*

### 20thC designs

Kosta's reputation for design improved after 1929 when Elis Bergh (1881–1954) was made art director. He helped to develop its reputation as one of the leading Swedish manufacturers. Many wares from this time feature simple shapes with engraved designs and internal ribs. Despite the successes of the art glass before the Second World War, the vintage postwar work is considered more collectable today.

### Marks

Kosta art glass is usually signed. However, most production glass is not signed, even if the design comes from a known designer. There was no uniform way of signing different pieces or series. This changed after Vicke Lindstrand's (see pp165–7) arrival as artistic director in 1950, when date codes and signatures were used for all the company's output.

*An early 20thC cameo glass vase, designed by Karl Lindeberg. 2.25in (5.5cm) high, H*

# 19thC Italian glass

Glass has been made in the Italian city of Venice since the 5thC AD. The city's glassmakers had travelled widely and *façon de Venise* ("Venetian-style") glassware was made throughout Europe. However, by the early 19thC many of the skills that had made Venetian glass desirable had been lost, and much of the glass made on the island of Murano was destined for domestic or pharmaceutical use as containers for oils and tinctures. At the same time, Venetian glassware was overshadowed by the new lead glass. But a group of craftsmen decided to reverse the fortunes of the city's glassmaking.

*A Salviati & Co. Venetian revival dolphin pitcher. c1890, 9.5in (24cm) high, G*

First, Abate Zanetti founded a glass museum on the island of Murano and, in 1862, a glass school there too. At the same time, craftsmen started to rediscover forgotten techniques and refine those that were not applied with the precision they had been used with in the past.

The designs that emerged paid tribute to the work of the past and were exhibited at exhibitions including the 1861 Florentine Exhibition and the 1880 Turin Exhibition. These included forms such as traditional *tazze*, serpent-stemmed drinking glasses and covered goblets. They also made chandeliers and mirror frames (the sheets of glass for the mirrors was imported).

• *Cristallo* glass, a colourless soda glass, that remained malleable for a long time after heating and so was particularly suited to elaborate shapes. Too thin and brittle for cut or carved decoration, *cristallo* glass was instead often embellished with diamond-point-engraved, enamelled or gilded decoration, or trailing.

• Glass intricately decorated with gilding, enamelling and trailing.

• *Filigrana* (or *latticinio*), a type of clear glass with a pattern of opaque white and coloured glass threaded or twisted into a design.
• Ice glass, the surface of which has a

*An enamel- and gilt-decorated footed bowl. c1880, 8in (20.5cm) diam, H*

cracked ice effect. First used in Venice in the 16thC, the surface decoration is created by plunging partially blown molten glass into cold water. Fissures form on the surface that then expand when the glass is gently reheated. Alternatively, the hot body is rolled in chips and canes, which are partially melted into the surface.
• The use of *murrines*, small slices of a coloured and patterned glass cane or rod typically arranged in a mosaic pattern over the surface of a vase, bowl or paperweight.
• Detailed decorative lampwork figures made from rods or tubes of glass that have been heated until

malleable and then moulded into intricate, delicate shapes.
• *Incalmo*, when two gathers of different colours are formed, blown, then joined at their open ends while still hot, fusing them together. The result is a single piece of glass with two different, distinct areas of colour. By the turn of the 20thC Venetian glass was regaining its popularity, thanks to the efforts of leading companies such as Salviati & Co. and Fratelli Toso (see pp176–7), and designers and makers such as Paolo Venini (1895–1959), Ercole Barovier (see pp172–3), Napoleone Martinuzzi (see pp174–5) and Carlo Scarpa (see pp178–9). They revived and introduced new forms, colours and decoration, much as the early Venetian glassmakers had done.

*A ruby glass goblet and dish, decorated with gilt. c1900, 14.25in (36cm) high, H*

# Ercole Barovier

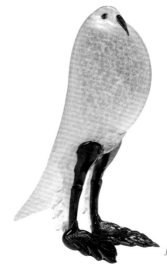

*A 1929 figure of a bird,
from the Primavera series.
12.5in (32cm) high, B*

1. Is the glass colourful?
2. Is it decorated with sections of coloured glass?
3. Does the glass have a white, crackled surface and black or blue trim?
4. Is the item made from thick glass and does it have an organic, textured shape?
5. Are pieces of silver foil trapped in the glass?
6. Is the marked engraved "Ercole" or "Barovier & Toso Murano" in script? Or is there a paper "Barovier & Toso" label?

### Ercole Barovier (1889–1974)

The Barovier family has been involved in glass production on the Venetian island of Murano since the 14thC. Four members of the family set up Fratelli Barovier in 1878 and built a reputation for producing colourful glass. In 1936 the company merged with another glassmaking dynasty and became known as Barovier & Toso in 1942. The tradition of making colourful glass continues, and Barovier remains a leading producer of Venetian glass.

### 20thC art glass

In 1919, Ercole Barovier gave up a career in medicine to join the company. He worked there for 53 years, during which he experimented

*An Art Deco cased glass vase, with bubbles and side decoration. 11in (28cm) high, E*

with new ways to bring colour and texture into glass. The techniques he used include:

• In the 1920s, decorating vessels with sections of coloured glass.

• The 1929 Primavera series, which had a distinctive white, crackled surface and black or blue trim that was the result of an accidental chemical combination and could not be repeated.

• A new technique he developed in the mid-1930s called *colorazione a caldo senza fusione* (colouring [glass] while hot without fusing). It was taken up by many other glassmakers.

• Organic, textured shapes in thick glass and others with trapped silver foil in the 1940s.

• "Primitive" shapes in the 1950s.

*A mosaic glass vase. c1930, 8.5in (21.5cm) high, D*

# Napoleone Martinuzzi

*A pulegoso vase, with applied loops at the sides, designed for Venini & Co. c1930, 14in (35.5cm) high, D*

1. Has the glass been formed into a sculptural shape?
2. Is the piece a traditional shape with unusual applied decoration?
3. Does the glass have a bubbly finish?
4. Is the glass opaque?
5. Is the glass marked with an acid-etched "Venini Murano" or "Made in Italy"? (Bear in mind that not all pieces are marked.)

## Napoleone Martinuzzi (1892–1977)

Napoleone Martinuzzi trained as a sculptor at the academy of fine art in Venice. In 1925 he was appointed artistic director of the Venini & Co. glassworks on Murano. Venini & Co became the leading post-war Italian glassworks. It produced decorative coloured glass,

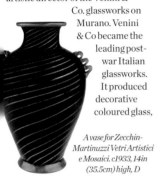

*A vase for Zecchin-Martinuzzi Vetri Artistici e Mosaici. c1933, 14in (35.5cm) high, D*

reviving many traditional Venetian techniques.

### Work for Venini & Co.

Initially Martinuzzi continued to work in the style of his predecessor Vittorio Zecchin (1878–1947), creating blown-glass objects. But soon he started to work in his own, sculptural, style.

The radical changes he brought included the use of more sculptural shapes (such as free-blown small animal sculptures), large plant

shapes and traditional forms with applied decoration, and technical breakthroughs including *pulegoso* (bubbly) glass.

Other changes were brought by Venini's cofounder Paolo Venini (1895–1959) and leading designers, including Gio Ponti (1891–1979) and Fulvio Bianconi (1915–1996). They also developed new glass forms and decoration. Examples created by Venini himself include the *pezzato* (patchwork) technique and the *fazzoletto* (handkerchief vase) form. In 1932, with Francesco Zecchin, he founded Zecchin-Martinuzzi Vetri Artistici e Mosaici where he made opaque and *pulegoso* glass.

*A pulegoso vase for Venini & Co. 1925–8, 10in (25.5cm) high, D*

# Fratelli Toso

*A "Kiku" murrine vase,
designed and made by
Ulderico Moretti. c1930,
9.5in (24cm) high, D*

1. Does the piece use *murrines* or *millefiori* fused with clear glass?
2. Have the *murrines* or *millefiori* been distorted by the glass-blowing process?
3. Is it a Classical-shaped vase made up of *murrines* or plain glass with applied handles?
4. Is the base signed with an incised signature "H. St. Lerche" for Hans Stoltenberg-Lerche?
5. Does the base have a round blue sticker that reads "MURANO GLASS MADE IN ITALY"?

## Fratelli Toso (1854–present)

In 1854 six brothers from the
Toso family founded a
glassmaking business
in Murano. They
revived the traditional
glassmaking skills
and, in 1864, created
a chandelier that was
given to the Murano
Glass Museum for its
inauguration.

The family went on
to find new ways to use
these traditional skills to
create vibrant and colourful

*A 1930s "Incamiciato" vase, the
purple handles decorated with
gold foil. 9.5in (24cm) high, G*

glass designs, many using *murrines*
and *millefiori* – slices of glass cane.

### Art Nouveau designs

In the early 1900s the factory made
elaborate glass in the *stile Liberty* –
the Italian Art Nouveau style. These
included Classical-shaped vases
made up of *murrines* fused with clear
glass and with applied handles.

### Modern designs

Before 1920, pieces by designers
including the German ceramicist
Hans Stoltenberg-Lerche

(1867–1920) were produced for
exhibitions such as the 1912 Venice
Biennale, rather than for sale.
This collaboration, which
lasted from 1910 until
1914, was the first between
Murano's glassblowers
an international artist.
Stoltenberg-Lerche's
glass designs featured
glass chips and metallic
powders. From the
1920s onwards, pieces
were made for retail
alongside a range of more
traditional forms which were
made for sale in the USA.

In 1924 Ermanno Toso
(1903–73) joined the
company, becoming artistic
director in 1936. He pioneered
the factory's
contemporary
art glass using
traditional
*murrines* and
*millefiori*.

*A "Murrine" vase,
white and black-blue
murrines with clear
glass. c1910, 4in
(10cm) high, G*

# Carlo Scarpa

*An a bugne vase, later factory signed "Venini Italia".*
*c1940, 12in (30.5cm) high, B*

1.  Does the glass feature layers of clear cased glass?
2.  Does the glass contain gold inclusions?
3.  Is there a matt, slightly iridescent surface to the glass?
4.  Is the surface of the glass the texture of hammered metal?
5.  Are the stripes in a spiral or do they resemble fabric?
6.  Is the glass an opaque milk-white?
7.  Is it decorated with *murrines*, prunts or swirls?
8.  Is the mark an acid stamp that reads: "VENINI MURANO MADE IN ITALY"?

## Carlo Scarpa (1906–78)

Born in Venice, Carlo Scarpa trained as an architect, but from 1934 until 1947 he worked as the artistic director of Venini & Co. (see p175). He later returned to architecture.

### New techniques

Scarpa initiated a highly productive period for Venini & Co. and introduced several decorative techniques that became hallmarks of the factory's output. These techniques and designs were still being made in the 1960s.

• *Sommerso*, a type of cased glass where a transparent, coloured core is enclosed by one or more differently

*A rectangular* sommerso a bolicine *vase. c1935, 4.75in (12cm) high, F*

coloured transparent layers of glass and a transparent, colourless, outer layer, which covers the entire body.

• *Sommerso a bollicine,* a form of cased glass with gold inclusions.

• *Corroso* glass, which has a distinctive matt, slightly iridescent surface.

• *Battuto,* a textured glass with a carved surface like hammered metal.

• Glass with spiralling stripes called *mezza filigrana.*

• Finely striped canes that created a fabric-like effect known as *tessuto.*

• An opaque milk-white glass referred to as *lattimo.*

• The square *occhi* vase, which was overlaid with a mosaic of *murrines.*

• Vases called *a bugne,* which had applied prunts or swirls.

### Marks

Scarpa's designs are acid-stamped: "Venini Murano Made in Italy" or "Venini Italia".

*A battuto vase, designed in 1940. 8in (20.5cm) high, E*

# American glass

Before the mid-18thC almost all American glass was imported and glass produced in the United States was considered to be experimental. A glass workshop was established at Jamestown, Virginia, in 1608, but it was forced to close by severe weather and unfavourable economic factors. The impetus for domestic glass production came following the American War of Independence (1775–7), when political ties with Britain were severed, and British imports halted. Another stimulus came from Irish and European immigrants, some of whom were skilled glassworkers. Many glasshouses were set up towards the end of the 18thC, and items produced were a mixture of European styles and designs. The most important of these were: the Wistarburgh glassworks near Alloway, New Jersey, built by Caspar Wistar (1692–1752) and the colonies' first successful glasshouse; the New Bremen glassworks established by John Frederick Amelung in Frederick County, Maryland, that was in operation for about ten years; and the glasshouses worked by Henry William Stiegel (1729–85) at Manheim, Pennsylvania, and the American Flint Glassworks. Early American glass included unrefined green glass (Stiegel) bottles, window glass and colourless tableware (Wistar), and English-style lead and non-lead stem and tableware. Decoration included enamelling, cutting and engraving. As well as producing tableware for everyday use, Amelung also made some commemorative engraved wares that are highly sought after.

In the early 19thC, the style of American glass moved away from the

*A New England blown olive-green glass deep bowl. c1800, 5.5in (14cm) diam, G*

*A blown-glass pan, with folded rim, probably Midwest. c1820, 7.75in (19.5cm) diam, F*

largely Bohemian influence, and after a brief "English" period went on to develop distinct forms and decorative techniques of its own.

The volume of glass made in the United States increased in every decade of the 19thC. In the 1820s, the American invention of making mechanically produced pressed glass (see pp210–11) revolutionized the mould-blowing technique. This made glass tableware, which had previously been affordable to only the very wealthy, within the reach of middle-class homes.

By the mid-19thC the American market had developed a taste for ornate styles and complex decorations. Among the products being made were art glass, candlesticks and lamps, and cut and engraved drinking glasses. However,

owing to the enormous home market, a large amount of glass was produced for functional, day-to-day use.

The pressed glass technique created pretty, decorative pieces, such as the Boston & Sandwich Glass Co. lacy glass (see pp186–7). This innovation quickly found its way back to Europe, and pressed glass was soon being made there.

The glassmaking areas of the USA were largely unaffected by the American Civil War (1861–15), but there were no further developments in styles or techniques. The period of unity and stability following the war facilitated an industrial revolution. Contact with Britain had been restored, and British glassmaking skills, finance and craftsmen were encouraged to come to the USA and develop new companies.

*A pair of mid-19thC Pittsburgh blown-glass milk pitchers. 7.5in (19cm) high, F (pair)*

The most famous examples of British influence over the American industry are the glassworks of Steuben (see pp194–5) and Hawkes (see pp206–7) in Corning, Massachusetts. Both factories had British founders or senior designers who had been head-hunted in England, and who went on to produce some of the best and most "American" glass ever made.

*A Stiegel-type blown-glass 16-rib creamer. c1800, 5in (12.5cm) high, G*

American companies that produced collectable pieces include the Mount Washington Glass Co. (see pp184–5) whose products include lamps, jugs, bowls and candlesticks in patented Burmese glass. The Steuben Glassworks (see pp194–5) produced high-quality, engraved crystal, Art Deco pieces including platters and stemware.

Bakewell Glassworks (1808–82) in Pittsburgh, PA, was renowned for its elaborate decoration, brilliance and its use of Irish designs and cutting patterns. The factory was founded by Benjamin Bakewell who became known as the "father" of American flint-glass. Until 1810 the Bakewell Glassworks was the only US factory producing this type of cut glass. In 1825, a very early patent for pressed glass was granted and production continued until the factory closed.

The Libbey Glass Co. (founded 1888), the biggest modern-day manufacturer of glass in America, was founded by William T. Libbey and his son, Edward Libbey, in Toledo, Ohio. It succeeded the New England Glass Co. and became known as Libbey in 1892. It specialized in transparent, cut and pressed lead glass and different types of coloured art glass – for example, Amberina and Peachblow. During the 1940s the company changed direction, moving away from art glass to mass-produced tableware, which is the main product still being made today.

The Boston & Sandwich Glass Co., the New England Glass Co. and the Washington Glass Co. all produced important paperweights. Probably the most famous name associated with the glass industry in the United States is Tiffany (see pp188–93). The Art Nouveau designs produced by Louis Comfort Tiffany in metal, jewellery and glass (and combinations of the three), are widely known and still copied throughout the world. Often "Tiffany" is used as a generic term describing a certain style, rather than a specific piece. Tiffany's father was a wealthy jeweller, and this gave him the chance to travel widely in Europe in his youth where he was influenced by the shapes and textures of ancient glass and early Art Nouveau. On his return to the United States he experimented with a variety

*The Night Shift, a painting by Leslie H. Nash depicting glassblowers at Tiffany Studios. 1924, 23in (58.5cm) wide, D*

of techniques and produced some highly distinctive wares, including lamps and vases.

Tiffany's iridescent glass inspired other American glassmakers, including Steuben, Quezal (see pp196–7) and Durand (see pp198–9) to make similar Art Nouveau wares. A simpler version of the finish was used on pressed Carnival glass (see pp212–15).

The skill of American glassmakers can also be seen in the lamps made by Tiffany, as well as companies such as Handel (see pp200–1) and Pairpoint (see pp202–3).

In the 1920s and 1930s, mass-produced, inexpensive, functional pressed glass, known as Depression glass, was particularly popular (see pp216–19).

*A New York or New Jersey blown-glass cup, with folded rim. c1830, 2.5in (6.5cm) high, F*

# Mount Washington Glass Co.

*A Royal Flemish vase, heavily decorated with winged dragon. c1890, 7.5in (19cm) high, E*

1. Does the satin-finished glass have enamelled decoration and a silver-plated mount?
2. Is the glaze similar to Chinese peach-bloom glaze, in shades of cream to light or deeper rose pink?
3. Does the glass have an opaque colour with a satin-like finish?
4. Does the glass have a light, semi-transparent body and a matt finish, decorated with gold and coloured enamel designs?
5. If the glass is marked, does it have a paper label or black or gold enamel mark such as "CM" and a crown, a round seal-style mark?

## Mount Washington Glass Co. (1837–1957)

This large glass manufacturer is best known for the art glass it produced from c1876 until the start of the 20thC. It was founded in South Boston, MA. In 1869, it moved to New Bedford under the control of William Libbey. In 1894, it was acquired by the metal company Pairpoint.

*A Burmese glass vase, painted with flowers. c1890, 11.75in (30cm) high, F*

### Wares

The glassworks specialized in satin-finished glass, with enamelled decoration and silver-plated mounts, which were made at nearby factories. It is best known for Peachblow, Burmese and Royal Flemish Art glass, as well as cut and cameo glass.

• Peachblow was made in imitation of Chinese peach-bloom glaze, in shades of cream to light or deeper rose pink.

• Burmese glass has a distinctive opaque colour with a satin-like finish (see also Thomas Webb, pp96–7). It

was invented in 1881 by Frederick Shirley and patented in 1885. Mount Washington used it for table glass and small decorative objects. Burmese glass with painted decoration has been increasingly popular in recent years, and values have risen.

• Royal Flemish is a decorative range of glass, with a light, semi-transparent glass body and a matt finish, decorated with intricate, gold and coloured enamel designs. It looks like stained glass sections separated by raised gilt lines. It was made from 1890 and patented in 1894. Patterns included Asian designs, birds and foliate and floral motifs.

### Marks

A lot of Mount Washington glass is unmarked. Others were marked with a paper label or black or gold enamel mark such as "CM" and a crown, a round seal-style mark.

*An acid-etched cameo glass vase. c1890, 8.75in (22cm) high, E*

185

# Boston & Sandwich Glass Co.

*A panelled paperweight perfume bottle,
smoky canary colour. c1840, 7.5in (19cm)
high, F*

1. Is the glass press-moulded glass with imperfections – small circles or dots – in the surface?
2. Has the pressed or blown glass been cased or cut?
3. Is the delicate glass finely blown and engraved?
4. Is the glass decorated with threading?
5. If a paperweight, is it similar in style to the work of Baccarat and Clichy (see pp134–5)?
6. Does the paperweight contain an 1852 date cane?
7. If a flower paperweight, is there a rose at the centre?

## The Boston & Sandwich Glass Co. (1826–88)

The Boston & Sandwich Glass Co. was founded by Deming Jarves (1760–1869) in 1826 at Sandwich, Cape Cod, MA. Jarves previously set up the New England Glass Co. (see pp210 and 221). In the 19thC it was one of North America's largest glassworks.

### Press-moulded wares

Sandwich was quick to utilize the new technology to make press-moulded glass. However, the moulds created imperfections – small dots – in the surface of the glass; detailed moulded decoration helped to disguise the flaws. These are called lacy glass.

### Cut- and cased wares

In the 1840s and 1850s, the company mass-produced a diverse range of practical and decorative wares. Pieces that were cut and blown in pressed and flashed (cased) glass. The designs were artistic and colourful in a "fancy" style,

*A 19thC poinsettia paperweight, in clear glass. 3in (7.5cm) diam, H*

known in the USA as Sandwich glass. As well as supplying the American home market, it exported wares to South America and the West Indies. In 1858 Jarves resigned and set up the Cape Cod Glass Works with his son John. He ran the company until his death in 1869.

### Engraved wares

By 1870 many more companies were producing less expensive pressed glass. As a result, by 1870, the Boston & Sandwich Glass Co. began to make delicate, finely blown and engraved glassware. At the same time, Frenchman Nicholas Lutz, who had served an apprenticeship at Saint-Louis, joined the company and introduced new styles, including threaded ware and paperweights. The factory closed in 1888 as a result of a national strike by glass workers.

*A late 19thC cut overlay fluid lamp, on a marble base. 20.5in (52cm) high, E*

# Tiffany Favrile glass

*A "Jack-in-the-Pulpit" vase, inscribed "L.C.T. 3059". c1900, 12.5in (32cm) high, AA*

1. Does the glass have an iridescent finish?
2. Is the piece an ornamental vase such as "Jack-in-the-Pulpit"?
3. Is it decorated with naturalistic plant and flower shapes?
4. Are the colours used gold and blue?
5. Are there any trailed or worked patterns?
6. Is it marked on the base with an etched or incised "Louis C. Tiffany" or "L.C.T." with a number?

## Louis Comfort Tiffany (1848–1933)

Son of the American jeweller Charles Tiffany, Louis Comfort visited Europe and the Middle East where he was inspired by decorative styles and forms from many countries. On his return he founded the Tiffany Glass & Decorating Co. in 1892, and

*An early Favrile vase, with leaves in "pulled feather" pattern. c1900, 17.75in (45cm) high, B*

in 1902 he became art director of his father's company, Tiffany & Co. He designed a wide variety of decorative wares (see pp190–3). Tiffany received international acclaim after he exhibited wares at the Exposition Universelle in Paris in 1900. Tiffany Studios closed in 1932.

## Favrile

Inspired by Roman and Islamic glass, and originally called Fabrile ("handmade"), Favrile was an iridescent glass patented in 1894.

• Different colours of glass were combined, then treated with metallic oxides and exposed to acid fumes.

• It was used in a wide selection of Art Nouveau glassware. The most common pieces were ornamental vases, often decorated with natural plant and floral shapes.

• Favrile glass is recognizable by the distinct gold and blue colours.

• The thickness of the underlying coloured glass determined the width and hue of iridescence.

• Trailed or worked patterns are rare.

*A Favrile vase, with blue leaves and opaline dogwood flowers. c1900–10, 6in (15.5cm) high, D*

189

# Tiffany lamps

*A "Dragonfly" table lamp, the shade with confetti "Favrile" glass forming the wings of the dragonflies. Shade dated 1913, base dated 1906, 20in (51cm) high, AAA*

1. Does the lamp have an Art Nouveau feel?
2. Does the ornamentation include naturalistic or floral motifs?
3. Does the piece have an organic, asymmetrical form?
4. Are the pieces of glass coloured and opaque with an iridescent surface?
5. Does the shade comprise hundreds of small pieces of glass?
6. Is there a small, marked tab on the inside of the shade?
7. Is there a number and a mark on the base?

## Tiffany lamps

Louis Comfort Tiffany (see pp188–9) began to produce lamps in around 1890. The shades were made from a large number of small pieces of his patented glass, Favrile (see pp188–9), or stained glass within a bronze framework. The bases, made from bronze or gilt bronze, were designed to resemble tree trunks.

Earlier pieces tended to be simple with geometric designs using only one or two colours. In time, decoration gradually became more complex and colourful. The glass was chosen for its ability to reproduce the colours found in nature.

*A rare and important "Wisteria Laburnum" leaded Favrile glass chandelier. c1910, 24in (61cm) diam, AAA*

Although patterns were used to make the lampshades, each was unique due to the individual pieces of glass.

### Styles of lamp

The lamp on p190 shows many typical features: a bronze, tree-trunk base, an intricate shade comprising hundreds of pieces of coloured glass, and a curved shape.

Hanging shades such as the "Wisteria Laburnum" example shown above were designed in an organic, asymmetrical style.

### Fakes and copies

• There are many copies of Tiffany's lamps, but these tend to have fewer, larger pieces of glass.

• All Tiffany lamps carry a copper tab on the inside of the shade, bearing the mark "TIFFANY STUDIOS NEW YORK", sometimes with a number. This is often overlooked by forgers.

*A 12-light gilt-bronze and Favrile glass "Lily" lamp. c1905, 21in (53cm) high, A*

# Other Tiffany glass

**Paperweight glass**

Here, the techniques used for making paperweights were transferred to vases. A piece of decorated glass was encased in a smooth outer layer that both protected and magnified the decoration. On some vases the flowers seem to be immersed in water that is trapped within the vase.

*A paperweight vase, with fine wheel-cut decoration. c1905, 6.25in (16cm) high, B*

**Cypriote glass**

Tiffany used many methods to try to recreate the natural decay seen on the surface of glass that had been buried since ancient times. A variation of Favrile (see pp188–9), Cypriote featured pitted, coloured, transparent yellow glass bodies that were rolled or marvered over crumbs of glass in blues, browns and greens, with a blue and purple iridescent sheen. Apart from the heavily textured surface, it featured minimal hand-formed decoration.

**Lava glass**

Lava glass was designed to resemble Lava or "volcanic" glass. Metallic oxides were mixed within the glass. This created an iridescent, gold "lava-flow" designed to mimic hot, molten rock erupting from the mouth of a volcano. Pieces of basalt or talc were added to the molten glass to create the rough, black areas of cooled lava. The glass was shaped into organic, irregular-shaped vases, jugs and other forms.

*A 1920s Cypriote vase with an original "The Tiffany Glass and Decorating Co." paper label. 7in (18cm) high, A*

*A Lava glass ewer. c1905, 4.5in (11.5cm) high, AAA*

## Aquamarine glass

This was the most difficult to make – and therefore the rarest and most valuable – of Tiffany's glass. It is a variation of the paperweight technique where the decoration was held between several layers of clear glass. The resulting glass is very heavy. The decoration usually features an underwater theme of aquatic plants, fish and other marine life such as sea urchins. The glass used to encase the decoration is green like the seas.

have been carved to create a naturalistic effect. The rim of the vase has been cut to show the clear glass beneath the layers of the colourful design.

*A Tiffany Studios carved overlay and internally decorated glass vase. c1910, 11.75in (30cm) high, B*

*An Aquamarine vase. 1911–12, 10in (25.5cm) high, A*

## Internally decorated glass

Tiffany enhanced the appearance of his glass designs by adding coloured glass to the exterior of the vessels and cutting and carving it to add more visual interest to the decoration. The result is a three-dimensional finish to flowers, leaves and other devices. On the example shown above right, the tulip petals, leaves and stems

## Stained glass

Before Tiffany, the techniques used to make leaded, stained glass had not changed since medieval times. His experiments allowed him to use more colours with richer hues. His

windows can be found in many of America's oldest colleges, among them Yale, Brown and Harvard.

*A "Lily" window, plated with up to three layers. c1915, 44in (112cm) high, AAA*

# Steuben Glassworks

*A 1920s rare red Aurene decorated vase, with gold iridescent leaf flower and vine decoration. 7.25in (18.5cm) high, B*

1. Does the glass have an iridescent finish?
2. Does the glass have a random, marbled finish?
3. Does the glass contain bubbles?
4. If the glass is clear, is it a colourless crystal glass?
5. Is the clear glass cut and engraved, possibly in an Art Deco style?
6. Is the glass in the style of an artist such as Henri Matisse or Salvador Dali?
7. Is the glass marked with an acid-stamped fleur-de-lys with "Steuben", or "Steuben" etched in script?

## Steuben Glassworks (1903–2011)

The Steuben Glassworks was established in 1903 by English glassmaker and chemist Frederick Carder (1863–1963) in Corning, New York. It was taken over by Corning Glass Works in 1918.

*An engraved "Gazelle" bowl, designed by Sidney Waugh. 1935, 7in (18cm) high, B*

### Wares

The factory produced a range of artistic lines, many of them in response to contemporary glassmakers. One of the most popular ranges was an iridescent glass called Aurene (made 1904–c33). Other ranges included Intarsia, Moss Agate and the bubbly Cluthra. In 1932, Steuben developed 10M: a pure, high-quality, colourless crystal glass, highly suitable for acid-etching, cutting and engraving. 10M soon dominated production, and coloured glass was discontinued in 1933.

### Designers

John Monteith Gates, George Thompson and the sculptor and architect Sidney Waugh (1904–63) were employed during the 1930s. Many of their designs were Art Deco in style. At the end of the 1930s, Steuben began to commission designs from artists, including Henri Matisse and Salvador Dali.

### Marks

From 1903–32 the marked was an acid-stamped fleur-de-lys with "Steuben" on a scroll. After 1932, it was "Steuben" etched in script.

*A Moss Agate vase, with bubbles and internal crackling. c1925, 10.5in (26.5cm) high, B*

# Quezal Art Glass & Decorating Co.

*A rare grape shade, decorated with purple grapes and green
lines against an opal background. c1920, 7in (18cm) high, E*

1. Is the glass relatively thick?
2. Is the design similar in quality and style to Tiffany?
3. Does the glass have a high-quality iridescent finish?
4. Is it decorated with a pulled-feather design?
5. Is the decoration subtle?
6. Is the glass marked with an engraved "Quezal"?
7. If it is a lamp, is it marked "Quezal" on the shades and the base?

### Quezal Art Glass & Decorating Co. (1901–25)

The Quezal glassworks was founded in Brooklyn, New York, by former Tiffany employees Thomas Johnson and Martin Bach. The company derived its name from its use of feather patterns similar to the brilliant green, red and white plumage of the South American quetzal bird.

Quezal made reproductions of Tiffany designs using a thicker glass but similar high-quality iridescent finish. It is best known for its use of pulled-feather decoration, which was more regular than similar decoration on Tiffany pieces. Undecorated pieces are rare. It also made lamps and lampshades. The quality of its glass make Quezal pieces popular and some early, unmarked pieces have been given Tiffany marks. After 1902 the glass was marked with "Quezal".

*A "Lily" lamp, with gold iridescent shades on a metal base. c1920, 18in (46cm) high, F*

### Kew Blas

The iridescent Kew Blas art glass range was produced by the Union Glass Company (1851–1924) of Somerville, MA, after about 1893. Before then the factory had specialized in clear cut, pressed and blown tableware and lamps. Kew Blas art glass was developed by factory manager William S. Blake (Kew Blas is an anagram of W. S. Blake). It was inspired by Quezal glass but the decoration is dramatic in comparison. Kew Blas used symmetrical shapes and the feathered decoration is clear and uses strong, brilliant colours.

Pieces are signed "Kew Blas" on the pontil mark.

*A vase with green and gold pulled-feather decoration on a creamy white background, interior gold finish. c1920, 8.25in (21cm) high, G*

# Durand

*A 1920s "King Tut" vase, iridescent blue finish with white and yellow vine decoration. 8.5in (21.5cm) high, F*

1. Does the glass have an iridescent "lustre" finish?
2. Has the inside been treated with a lustre finish as well as the outside? If so, they may not be the same colour.
3. Is the style of the piece regular and simple?
4. Does the decoration include random trails of glass thread, random drips of colour, cameo and other cut designs?
5. Does the pattern look like random swirls or peacock feathers?
6. Is the glass finish deliberately crackled?
7. Is the piece signed "Durand"? Is the lettering across a letter "V"?

## Durand (1924–32)

Durand glass was a range of art glass made at the Vineland Glass Manufacturing Co. in Vineland, New Jersey. The works was founded by Frenchman Victor Durand Jnr (d.1931) and his father Victor

*A 1920s squat vase, with "Lady Gay Rose" coral red striped decoration. 10.5in (26.5cm) diam, E*

Durand Snr in 1897. The son had worked for the Baccarat glassworks in France before emigrating to the USA in 1884.

### Wares

The company's first products were industrial and scientific glasswares but, thanks to their success, the factory's range was expanded to include art glass in 1924. Martin Bach Jr, a cofounder of Quezal and former employee of Tiffany, was employed to design a range of mainly iridescent "lustre"

glass. The finish was often used on the inside as well as the outside of the glass. The factory used regular and simple forms.

### Decoration

Decoration included random trails of glass thread called "spider-webbing", random drips of colour, cameo and other cut designs. Noted patterns include the random swirled "King Tut" and the "Peacock Feather". From 1925, the company also produced lamp bases and crackle glass with names such as "Moorish Crackle" and "Egyptian Crackle". In 1931–2, the company merged with the Kimble Glass Company and the art glass department was closed.

### Marks

Early cut glass is usually unmarked. Later pieces are signed "Durand", the lettering sometimes across the letter V.

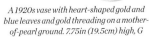

*A 1920s vase with heart-shaped gold and blue leaves and gold threading on a mother-of-pearl ground. 7.75in (19.5cm) high, G*

# Handel Lamps

*An early 20thC rare "Peacock lamp", the reverse and obverse painted shade with cameo peacock with flowing tail feathers and gold iridescent finish. 24.5in (62cm) high, B*

1. Is the decoration on the glass lampshade painted on the reverse?
2. Is the shade painted or enamelled with scenic views or flora on the interior and finished on the exterior with a frosted or "chipped ice" finish?
3. Does the metal base complement the subject on the shade?
4. Is the shade a hemisphere, cone, dome, cylinder or loaf-shaped?
5. Does the shade have a painted mark and four-figure design number on the inside of the base?
6. Is the shade with marked "Handel Lamps" and a patent number on the metal rim at the top?

## Handel Company (1885–1936)

The Handel Company was founded in Meriden, Connecticut, in 1885, by Philip J. Handel (1867–1914) and Adolph Eydam. It was initially called Eydam & Handel and renamed The Handel Company in 1903 after Handel bought out his partner.

### Wares

Handel specialized in decorating reverse-painted glass lampshades. Typically, these are hemispherical in shape, painted or enamelled with scenic views or flora on the interior and finished on the exterior with a

*An early 20thC table lamp, with a chipped glass shade, reverse-painted by Peter Broggi with birds and flowers. 23in (58.5cm) high, C*

frosted finish or a "chipped ice" finish, which diffused the light well. Other styles include cone, dome, cylindrical and loaf-shaped desk lamps.

The painted designs included birds, flowers, leaves or butterflies; or landscapes and seascapes, some with Egyptian or tropical scenes.

### Marks

Shades usually have a painted mark and four-figure design number on the inside of the base of the shade. Some also have a designer's name. After 1910 shades were usually impressed with "Handel Lamps" and a patent number on the metal rim at the top.

### Value

The appeal, and value, lies in the decoration of the shade. Today, rare designs can compete with some Tiffany lamps in value.

*An early 20thC lamp, with an etched glass shade reverse-painted. 23.5in (59.5cm) high, C*

# Pairpoint Lamps

*A 1920s Puffy "Azalea" lamp, the shade decorated with azaleas against a leafy background. 19in (48cm) high, C*

1. Has the lampshade been reverse-painted with a landscape?
2. Is the shade ribbed or does it feature floral decoration in high relief?
3. Is the base made from bronze, copper or silver plate?
4. Does the design of the base complement the shade?
5. Are the base and shade marked "Pairpoint Mfg. Co. 3095" with the Pairpoint logo and/or with a patent number?
6. Has the shade been signed by the designer?

## Pairpoint Corporation (1880–1957)

The Pairpoint Corporation was founded in New Bedford, Massachusetts. It was a metalware company that produced functional and decorative household items. Pairpoint would then go on to become a leading producer of reverse-painted glass lampshades. Many of its products were combined with glass made by the Mount Washington Glass Co. (see pp184–5). In 1894, the companies merged and the new company's products met with great success until the 1929 Depression. The metalware company closed in 1937 due to continued financial problems and more competitive imports.

*A 1920s table lamp, the shade reverse-painted with a woodland scene. 20in (51cm) high, E*

## Wares

Pairpoint is best known for its scenic lampshades, ribbed designs and the Puffy range, such as the lamp shown on p 202, which featured flower decoration in high relief.

The bases were made from a variety of metals, including bronze, copper and silver plate. The design of the base usually complemented the shade, but customers were able to choose from a range of bases which would fit the shades.

## Marks

Pairpoint shades and bases are usually marked, and sometimes signed by the designer.

*An unusual 1920s lamp, with scenes of exotic birds in a natural habitat. 21in (53cm) high, E*

# Other glass lamp manufacturers

**Bradley & Hubbard Manufacturing Co.**

In 1854 brothers-in-law Walter Hubbard and Nathaniel Lyman Bradley set up a company in Meriden, Connecticut, to make cast-iron wares. At the beginning of the 20th C it started to make lamps with reverse-painted shades. The firm was bought by the Charles Parker Company in 1940.

*A Bradley & Hubbard lamp with reverse-painted shade. c1900, 22in (56cm) high, F*

**Moe-Bridges**

The Moe-Bridges Co. was based in Milwaukee, Wisconsin and made lamps with reverse-painted shades inspired by

*A 1920s Moe-Bridges reverse-painted table lamp. 22.5in (57cm) high, E*

Handel (see pp200–1) and Pairpoint (see pp202–3). The decoration often featured landscapes or flowers. Its lamps were not of the same quality as those it emulated. The bases tended to be patinated iron rather than the bronze used for high-quality lamps.

**Duffner & Kimberly**

The Duffner & Kimberly Co. was formed in New York in 1905 by Oliver Speers Kimberly, who had worked for Tiffany

*A Duffner & Kimberly table lamp, with leaded-glass shade in the Louis XV pattern. c1910, 29.5in (75cm) high, A*

Studios in the 1890s, and Frank Duffner. The company made a relatively small number of stained glass lamps of a similar quality to Tiffany. Designs tend to feature patterns rather than naturalistic designs. It closed c1911.

*A 1920s Gorham table lamp, with a leaded-glass shade of cyclamen. 22.5in (57cm) high, D*

## Gorham Manufacturing Co.

Gorham is the largest American silversmiths and was founded in 1818 in Providence, Rhode Island. From 1905 it also made elaborate leaded lampshades on bronze bases, which rivalled those made by Tiffany for the quality of their design and manufacture.

## Jefferson Lamp Co.

The Jefferson Lamp Co. was founded in 1900 in

*A 1920s Jefferson lamp, the shade reverse-painted with a landscape. 22in (56cm) high, E*

Steubenville, Ohio. Seven years later the company moved to Follansbee, Virginia, where it produced reverse-painted lamps until it closed in 1933. The lamps are of a high quality and decorated with landscape, floral and Art Deco designs.

*A 1920s Suess table lamp, with leaded-glass shade on a tree-trunk base. 23in (58.5cm) high, C*

## Suess Ornamental Glass Co.

The Chicago-based Suess Ornamental Glass Co. was active from 1886 until 1910. Its lamps are relatively rare. It made naturalistic or geometric-patterned shades from leaded glass and may feature sections of iridescent glass. The overall design and quality of Suess' lamps is very similar to those made by Tiffany. The company closed following a fire.

# T. G. Hawkes & Co.

*A late 19thC rare engraved and cut-glass bowl, with dragon decoration, by Edward Palme. 9in (23cm) diam, E*

1. Is the cutting on the glass so deep it is almost too prickly to touch?
2. Has the glass been given a highly polished finish?
3. Does the design combine cutting and engraving on a heavy crystal body?
4. Does the glass ring like a bell when it is struck gently?
5. Is the base marked with two hawks and a fleur-de-lys inside a trefoil? The mark may be acid-etched or on a paper label.
6. Has the base been signed by the designer?

## T. G. Hawkes & Co. (1880–1962)

T. G. Hawkes & Co, of Corning, New York, was among the glass companies set up at the end of the 19thC to meet the growing demand for cut glass from middle-class households. Thomas G. Hawkes (1840–1913) had emigrated from Ireland in 1867 and worked for other companies before setting up his own. At the turn of the 20thC it was one of the largest glassmakers in the United States.

### "Brilliant" glass

The period of 1876–1914 is known as the "Brilliant" period of American glassmaking as much of the glass made was decorated with deep

*A pair of cut-glass decanters in an American silver tantalus stand. c1910–40, 10in (25.5cm) high, G*

*A late 19thC rare goblet, engraved by William H. Morse. 7.5in (19cm) high, AA*

cutting and highly polished finish. Hawkes' glass could be so deeply cut it was almost too prickly to touch.

### Wares

Hawkes produced flamboyant decorative and tablewares which combined cutting and engraving on heavy crystal bodies. One of its most celebrated and deeply cut patterns was the "Russian" cut, introduced in 1882 for a service commissioned by the Russian Embassy in Washington. A second service was made for the White House in 1885. In 1889 two of its cut-glass patterns won the Grand Prix at the Paris Exhibition.

### Marks

After 1895 all pieces were marked with two hawks and a fleur-de-lys inside a trefoil.

# Pairpoint Corporation

*A 1920s "Fine Arts" covered vase, with silver-plated mounts. 13in (33cm) high, F*

1. Is the glass a piece of tableware or lighting made from coloured or colourless clear glass?
2. Does it feature engraved or cut decoration, or a combination of the two?
3. Is there complex applied decoration such as silver, threading and swirls?
4. Does the glass have a silver-plated mount?
5. Is the glass marked "Pairpoint", "The Pairpoint Corporation" or with "PMC" within a diamond?

## Pairpoint Corporation (1880–1957)

In 1880 the Mount Washington Glass Co. (see pp184–5) set up the Pairpoint Manufacturing Co. in New Bedford, Massachusetts, to produce silver-plated mounts for its glass. It was run by English silversmith Thomas J. Pairpoint.

The companies were combined in 1894 and renamed the Pairpoint Corporation in 1900. At about 1900, the factory employed more than 1,000 workers, but by 1938, only 20 employees were left and work had stopped. It closed in 1938, re-opening as the Gundersen-

*A "Marina Blue" two-handled glass urn. 1910–20, 12in (30.5cm) high, H*

*A Rosaria "Lincoln" pattern vase, with block base. 1910–20, 13.5in (34.5cm) high, F*

Pairpoint Glass Company until 1957. A small glass firm named Pairpoint now exists in Sagamore, Massachusetts, but it has no direct connection to the original company.

### Wares

Pairpoint flourished from 1880 until 1930 when the Depression hit, and was a rival to Tiffany and Steuben. From c1910 until c1930 it made tablewares and lighting in a variety of styles. Most of the wares were made from coloured or colourless clear glass, often with engraved or cut decoration, or a combination of the two. Others featured applied coloured decoration including silver, threading and swirls in the glass. Some of these styles and decorating techniques are so complex they are rarely used today.

# North American pressed glass

The technique of "pressing" glass – shaping it by pouring molten glass into a mould and then pressing down with a plunger to create a smooth interior surface and a mould-patterned exterior – was developed in the USA from the 1820s. It allowed factories to mass-produce inexpensive copies of fashionable cut-glass designs.

Before the 1820s, moulded glass was made by blowing a gather of molten glass into a mould. One of the most celebrated craftsmen was German-born Henry William Stiegel (1729–85) who produced high-quality blue, purple, green and crystal-clear glassware. He arrived in Philadelphia in 1750, and by 1760 he was one of the most prosperous ironmasters in the country. He also made window glass and bottles and employed Venetian, German and English glass workers.

The Boston & Sandwich Glass Co. was probably the most important American pressed glass manufacturer (see pp186–7). Another well-known maker was the New England Glass Co. (1817–88), which was originally based in East Cambridge, Massachusetts. It developed the first glass-pressing machine and is best known for its Amberina and Pomona lines. The company was founded in 1817, by Deming Jarves and others, on their purchase of the Boston Porcelain & Glass Manufacturing Co. factory (founded in 1814).

Throughout the 19thC, the New England Glass Co. made useful and ornamental wares including paperweights, much of it created by immigrant artisans from Europe. From the mid-19thC the company

*A Stiegel moulded flask, in a diamonds-above-flute pattern. c1770, 5in (12.5cm) high, E*

introduced numerous artistic lines, notably Amberina and Pomona, developed by Joseph Locke. The company moved to Toledo, Ohio, in 1888 and, as the Libbey Glass Co. (see p182) specialized in transparent, cut and pressed lead glass and different types of coloured art glass, for example Amberina and Peachblow. During the 1940s it changed direction, moving away from traditional art glass to mass-produced tableware, which is the main product still being made today. Another company famed for its pressed glass is the Phoenix Glass Co., founded in 1880 in Phillipsburg

*A late 19thC New England Glass Co. pressed Amberina vase, by Joseph Locke. 4.5in (11.5cm) high, F*

(now Monaca), Pennsylvania. It made lampshades, bottles and other glassware but collectors focus on the art glass made by Joseph Webb, Jnr, the cousin of an English glassmaker, Thomas Webb, from 1883 to 1894 and the Sculptured Artware made from the 1930s until the mid-1950s. The Phoenix Glass Co. is still in operation today.

By the 1850s a number of pressed glass companies had been founded across the Midwest. At this time most inexpensive mass-produced glassware – such as iridescent Carnival glass (see pp212–15) and clear Depression glass (see pp216–19) – was pressed.

*A 1930s Phoenix Glass blue pressed glass "Freesia" vase. 8.25in (21cm) high, I*

# Fenton

### Fenton (1905–present)

The Fenton family business began as a glass decorating workshop in Martin's Ferry, Ohio. In 1906 the company's founders – brothers Frank Leslie (1880–1948) and John W. Fenton (1869–1934) – built a glass factory in Williamstown, West Virginia, and a year later the Fenton Art Glass Co. launched Iridill, a range of press-moulded, iridescent wares. By 1908 the glass – sometimes

*A 1930s "Dragon and Lotus" pattern blue Carnival glass bowl. 8.5in (21.5cm) diam, I*

called "poor man's Tiffany" was being mass-produced. It became known as Carnival glass in the 1950s when it had fallen out of fashion and was often given away as a funfair prize.

### Wares

Fenton's most popular patterns include "Peacock and Grape" and "Dragon and Lotus". It used a wide range of colours, such as royal blue, purple, marigold and green. A red glass, introduced in the 1920s, was complicated to make and pieces are rare – and valuable – today. The Hobnail range was launched by Fenton in 1938. Many shapes and colours were produced as experimental short runs – with some hand-finishing – and these are popular with collectors, as are crisply moulded pieces made from new moulds.

*A 1930s "Orange Tree" pattern marigold Carnival glass hat pin stand. 6.5in (16.5cm) high, I*

### Reproductions

In the 1960s and 1970s the demand for vintage Carnival glass lead Fenton to make reproduction pieces using the original moulds. All these news pieces are marked "Fenton" in script in an oval cartouche. Early Carnival pieces are often unmarked.

# Northwood

**The Northwood Glassworks
(1887–1925)**
Established in Martin's Ferry, Ohio, it
was one of Fenton's (see p212) major
competitors. It was founded by Harry
Northwood, the son of leading British
glassmaker John Northwood, who

*A 1920s "Grape & Cable" pattern amethyst
Carnival glass butter dish and cover.
6in (15.5cm) high, I*

had emigrated to the United States six
years before. He relocated the company
to Indiana, Pennsylvania, in 1895. It
began making iridescent glass in 1902
following a move to Wheeling, West
Virginia. The Carnival glass, which
was to become its most successful
range, was first made in 1908.

**Wares**
Collectors look for punchbowl sets
and plain, flat plates, which show off
the patterns. "Grape & Cable" was

one of its most popular patterns. It
is found on more than 40 different
objects in colours such as blue, green,
orange, marigold and amethyst; rare
colours are smoke, amber and grey
blue. The crisp, deeply moulded
patterns were often hand-finished.
Bowls with wavy, hand-crimped
edges were popular, as was the "Good
Luck" motto-ware bowl (see below).
The quality of the iridescence, and
rarity of the colour, determine value.

**Marks**
Many pieces are marked with an
underlined "N", usually set in a circle.
but occasionally without a circle or
inside a double circle.

*A 1920s "Good Luck" pattern marigold Carnival
glass ruffled bowl. 8.75in (22cm) diam, I*

# Other Carnival glass

### Diamond Glass Co. (1913–31)

The Diamond Glass Co. was founded when Thomas Dugan left the Dugan Glass Co. (see below). It produced

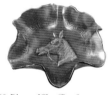

*A 1920s Diamond Glass "Pony" pattern, marigold Carnival glass bowl. 8.25in (21cm) diam, I*

Carnival glass until 1931, introducing new patterns such as "Golden Harvest", "Peacock at the Fountain", "Windflower", "Stork in the Rushes", "Double Stemmed Rose", "Pony and "Weeping Cherry". A major fire forced the factory to close.

### Dugan Glass Co. (1904–13)

Thomas Dugan was a cousin of Harry Northwood (see p213) who managed his factory in Indiana, Pennsylvania. In 1904 Dugan, with the help

*A Dugan "Raindrops" pattern, peach opalescent ruffled bowl. c1910, 8.25in (21cm) diam, I*

of investors, purchased the glass plant and founded the Dugan Glass Co. It produced Carnival glass from 1909 and made marigold, amethyst, peach-opal and white glass, plus a little green and blue. Designs included "Persian Gardens" and "Apple Blossom Twigs". In 1913 it became the Diamond Glass Co (left).

*An 1880s Gillinder & Co. Amberina pressed glass dish, part of a set. 5.5in (14cm) long, I*

### Gillinder & Co. (1861–c1930)

The Gillinder & Co. glassworks in Philadelphia, Pennsylvania, and later New Jersey, made many different types of glass, including pressed, frosted and coloured examples. Its founder William T. Gillinder first made pressed glass in 1863 and ten years later began to use acid-etched decoration.

## Imperial Glass Co. (1901–85)

This glassworks was founded in Bellaire, Ohio, with the aim of producing affordable, high-quality glass. In 1910 it started to sell Carnival glass that

*An early 20thC Imperial "Ripple" pattern, amethyst Carnival glass vase. 12in (30.5cm) high, I*

was designed to be functional and decorative. Production of iridescent wares slowed in the 1950s but pieces were reissued in the 1960s to meet demand. The factory closed in 1985.

## Jeanette Glass Co. (1887–1983)

The Jeanette Glass Co. is best known for its Depression glass (see

*A 1930s "Windsor Diamond" butter dish, by Jeanette Glass Co. 6in (15.5cm) diam, I*

pp218–19) but also made some Carnival glass. The factory was based in Jeannette, Pennsylvania, and began to produce glass tablewares in the early 1920s. By 1927 all hand-production had ceased as it was one of the first factories to install fully automatic production.

## Millersburg (1908–11)

The Millersburg Glass Co. was founded by John Fenton (see p212) and produced some of the most desirable Carnival glass designs.

*A Millersburg "Mayan" pattern, green Carnival glass bowl. c1910, 8.5in (21.5cm) diam, I*

It used amethyst, green and a soft marigold glass; early pieces had a soft satin finish, but soon a high-gloss "radium" finish was introduced. Patterns include "Ohio Star", "Holly Sprig", "Night Stars" and "Sunflower".

# Hazel-Atlas Glass Co.

*A "Royal Lace" green Depression glass
cookie jar. 1934–41, 7.5in (19cm) high, I*

1. Is the piece made from plain or coloured pressed glass?
2. Is it decorated with a traditional floral or foliate patterns or was it
   made in the Art Deco style?
3. Is it a functional item, such as a jug, bowl, drinking glass or plate?
4. Is the colour transparent blue, green, pink or crystal, or opaque
   black?
5. Is it marked with an "A" below an "H"?

## Hazel-Atlas Glass Co. (1902–56)

The company known today as the Hazel-Atlas Glass Co. was founded in 1902 in Washington, Pennsylvania, with the merger of four companies: Hazel Glass and Metals Co., Atlas Glass Co., Wheeling Metal Plant and Republic Glass Co. At one time it was the largest glass manufacturer in the world.

*A "Royal Lace" cobalt blue twin-handled cup. 1934–41, 4.25in (11cm) high, I*

### Depression glass

The company first made the inexpensive, pressed glass known as Depression glass in the early 1920s. It was one of a number of companies who made it in a huge range of styles and colours. It was often used as promotional offers in stores. The glass was machine-made and available in a vast number of patterns and colours, from traditional floral or foliate patterns to Art Deco styles. Most was functional, including jugs, bowls, drinking glasses and plates.

### Wares

The Hazel-Atlas Glass Company's first Depression glass was the "Ovide" dinnerware pattern launched in 1923. It was produced in a transparent green or opaque black. The "Royal Lace" pattern was produced from 1934 until 1941. The colours made included blue, green, pink and crystal, though only crystal was produced throughout the life of the pattern. Today, blue "Royal Lace" is one of the most desirable Depression glass patterns.

### Marks

Most pieces produced after 1923 are marked with an "A" below an "H".

*A "Royal Lace" green salt shaker, with metal top. 1934–41, 4in (10.5cm) high, I*

# Other Depression glass

### Cambridge Glass Co. (1873–1958)

*A 1920s Cambridge Glass Company Draped Lady centrepiece. 12.5in (31.5cm) high, I*

The Cambridge Glass Co. was founded in Cambridge, Ohio. It made coloured glassware in the 1920s, initially in opaque shades such as helio, jade, primrose, azurite and ebony, but changing to pale, transparent glass by the end of the decade.

### Fostoria Glass Co. (1887–1986)

This factory was founded in Fostoria, Ohio. It eventually

*A late 19thC Fostoria "American" pattern crystal beer mug. 1915–86, 4.75in (12cm) high, I*

moved to Wheeling, West Virginia, and then to Moundsville, West Virginia. In 1915 it began to produce the "American" pattern, which it made until it closed in 1986. During the Depression its glass was still of high quality, especially in comparison with its competitors' products.

*A 1930s–40s Hocking Glass Co. "Block Optic" pattern green juicer. 6in (15.5cm) diam, I*

### Hocking Glass Co. (1905–2014)

Hocking, which became Anchor Hocking in 1937, was one of the biggest names in Depression glass.

During the 1930s, Hocking was able to produce 90 items a minute, which meant it could sell a pair of tumblers for a nickel. Collectors pay a premium for Depression-era Hocking in rare colour and pattern combinations or designs.

## Indiana Glass Co. (1907–2002)

The Indiana Glass Co. of Dunkirk, Indiana, was formed in 1907 following a merger of other glass factories. It made pressed and blown glass lamps and press-moulded decorative plates and bowls. From c1925 until 1940 it made Depression glass in patterns such as "Avocado", "Horseshoe", "Lorain", "Old English", "Pineapple and Floral", "Pyramid" and "Tea Room". Glass is still made using the Indiana Glass Co. name.

*An Indiana goblet in the "Sandwich Daisy" pattern. c1930, 5.5in (14cm) high, I*

## Jeanette Glass Co. (1887–1983)

The Jeanette Glass Co. of Jeanette, Pennsylvania (see also p215) launched the first complete range of tablewares in 1928, using amber, green, pink and topaz glass. Two years later it produced the first complete line of moulded tableware

*A 1930s pink candlestick in the "Adam" pattern by the Jeannette Glass Company. c1940, 3.75in (9.5cm) high, I*

in a choice of three colours: pink, apple green and crystal. Depression glass patterns included "Jenny", "Windsor Diamond" and "Adam".

## New Martinsville Glass Co. (1901–44)

Founded in New Martinsville, West Virginia, it made tableware and novelties such as animal figurines and bookends. Its Depression glass patterns included "Raindrops", "Queen Anne", "Modernistic", "Moonstone" and "Radiance". It used colours such as amber, ruby, green, amethyst, blue, pink, black and yellow.

In 1941 it began to make Viking Crystal. Sold in 1944, it was renamed the Viking Glass Co.

*A 1930s New Martinsville "Moondrops" tumbler. 4.75in (12cm) high, I*

# Other American glass

**Clevenger Brothers (1930–66)**
The Clevenger brothers – Henry Thomas (Tom), Lorenzo (Reno) and William Elbert (Allie) – worked at the Moore Brothers factory in Clayton until it closed in 1912. They tried to find alternative work but eventually, in 1930, opened their own glassmaking business. From their backyard they made reproductions of early American glassware. Some pieces were made from pressed glass, while others were mould- or free-blown. Their wares included bowls, double-handled vases and mugs. The pieces tend to be heavier than the originals and in more vibrant colours than those used by early glassmakers. The company was sold in 1966 and the glassworks closed in 1999.

*A 1940s Clevenger Brothers free-blown vase. 8.75in (22cm) high, I*

**Handel Co. (1885–1936)**
As well as the reverse-painted lampshades for which it is famous, the Handel Co. (see also pp200–1) produced a line of vases that are rarely seen today. There were three types: acid-etched clear and yellow glass (see example above); the Tremona line, which feature an ice-chipped surface and painted enamel decoration; and early, ice-chipped painted vases that feature large-scale decoration.

*A Handel cameo vase, signed "GUBISCH". c1900, 10in (25.5cm) high, G*

**A. H. Heisey & Co. (1895–1957)**
German-born Augustus Heisey (1842–1922) worked as a glass salesman before setting up his own company in Newark, Ohio, in 1895. Production started in 1896 and Heisey went on to employ nearly 700 people who made high-quality glassware that was sold around the

world. Coloured glass was made in the 1920s and 1930s, and glass figurines in the 1940s and 1950s. Foreign competition and increasing costs were among the reasons for the company's closure in 1957.

**New England Glass Co. (1817–88)**
The New England Glass Co. (see also pp187 and 210) was founded by Deming Jarves and others. Its mid-19thC Art glass included the

*A late 19thC New England Glass Co. Amberina glass carafe. 8.25in (21cm) high, G*

Its ranges included mother of pearl with finishes such as rainbow, diamond, spot, drape and ribbed panel optic; Peachblow glass (also known as mandarin), acid-etched cameo glass and cased glass.

*A 1930s Heisey mould-blown ball vase. 5.75in (14.5cm) high, I*

Amberina and Pomona ranges, developed by Joseph Locke. The company moved to Toledo, Ohio, in 1888 and, as the Libbey Glass Co., is still in existence.

**Phoenix Glass Co. (1880–present)**
The Phoenix Glass Co. (see also p211) is best remembered today for the art glass made by Joseph Webb, Jnr

*A Phoenix Glass Co. apricot glass vase, with airtrap decoration. 1880–90, 8.25in (21cm) high, H*

221

# Chinese glass

The first glass made in China dates from the reign of the Manchu Emperor K'ang Hsi (1661–1727) who was influenced by Western missionaries. At that time, a variety of glasswares were produced, including plain and coloured clear and opaque glass, carved and overlay glass, and white enamelled glass made to imitate porcelain.

*A fine 18thC "Imperial" incised yellow glass vase, Qianlong mark. 8.25in (21cm) high, D*

A workshop attached to the Emperor's palace in Beijing was established in 1696. It was run by Kilian Stumpf, a German Jesuit priest who was also a glassmaker. He worked with Chinese craftsmen from Shandong in north-west China

or Guandong and Suzhou in the south. A combination of Chinese and European skills were still being used in the 1740s and 1750s when Jesuits with glassmaking skills are also known to have been working in the palace workshops.

The items they made in the workshops included vases, cups, bowls, snuff bottles, incense burners and items for the scholar's desk. These were used in the palace or given as presents.

## Coloured glass

Many types of plain and coloured glass were produced in China, and were popular because of their resemblance to the colours of precious stones and mineral deposits. Blue glass was popular because it resembled lapis lazuli, and red and yellow glass was favoured because it looked like realgar, a mineral containing arsenic.

Possibly the most well-known single colour among Chinese glasswares is "Imperial yellow", which echoed the yellow-glazed porcelain used exclusively by the Emperor and his family. The incised vase of tall baluster form shown on the left illustrates the characteristic rich, egg-yolk yellow was made exclusively for the court. It also has a typical flared rim over a waisted neck and tapering foot. The body of the vase is decorated with rows of detailed Chinese script.

## Chinese overlay glass

The best known Chinese glass are cameo pieces with a coloured overlay and opaque white ground. They were made to resemble precious stones and the carving is considered to be distinctly oriental in style. It is likely that craftsmen experienced in carving jade with a wheel and abrasives transferred their skills to glass.

*A 18th/19thC opaque white glass bowl, with blue glass overlay. 6in (15.5cm) diam, H*

Initially red and clear or "snowflake" white glass were more commonly used for Chinese overlay wares. Other colour combinations soon became popular, such as this white and blue bowl (above), which imitated blue and white porcelain, and even multi-coloured overlay or "marquetry".

## Collecting

• Chinese glass is still made by hand, so be careful when evaluating pieces – it can be difficult to distinguish between old and new examples.

• The value of Chinese glass is determined more by quality than age. Wear is not a reliable indicator of age because many pieces were made simply for display.

• Copying in China is considered to be a mark of respect – even down to signatures and marks: take care when evaluating any piece.

*An 18thC "apple green" vase. 8.5in (21.5cm) high, H*

# Beijing glass

*A 19thC Beijing overlaid glass bottle vase.*
*7.75in (20.5cm) high, D*

1. Is the item made up of several layers of coloured glass with the outer layers carved to create a design?
2. Is the piece a single colour of glass with carved or incised decoration?
3. Is it a snuff bottle, vase, bowl or jar?
4. Is there a four- or six-character Chinese reign mark on the base?
5. Is it decorated with a traditional Chinese subject such as flowers, landscapes, religious symbols, people, birds, dragonflies, grasshoppers or horses?
6. Are there signs that it was moulded rather than handmade? If so it is a modern piece.

## Beijing glass

The term "Beijing glass" usually refers to the overlaid, carved glass that has been made in the city since the early Qing Dynasty in the late 17thC (see p222). It is sometimes

*An 18thC Beijing zhadou vase. 4.25in (11cm) high, F*

called "Peking" glass, after the old Western name for the city. Like European cameo glass, several layers of coloured glass are carved to create a design. At first, it was only used for snuff bottles (see pp226–7), but later examples include vases, bowls and jars. Other glass made in Beijing includes single-colour pieces, sometimes with carved decoration.

### Qianlong Period

The finest pieces date from the Qianlong Period (1736–95) and the most valuable of these are snuff bottles. By this time, snuff was a social practice among the wealthy. Carved glass snuff bottles are so strongly associated with the time that the term "Qianlong" is often used instead of Beijing glass.

### Decoration

Designs include classic Chinese subjects such as flowers, landscapes, religious symbols and people. Birds, dragonflies, grasshoppers and horses are also popular subjects.

### Collecting

Beijing glass is still being made and may even bear the same marks. Historic pieces were handmade so any signs that a piece was moulded mean it is unlikely to be authentic.

*A pair of 18thC Beijing vases with red overlay on yellow. 7.75in (20.5cm) high, F*

225

# Chinese snuff bottles

The Chinese were introduced to the practice of taking snuff (sniffing powdered tobacco) by European visitors, and the habit was fashionable at the Chinese court by the 1680s. While Europeans kept their snuff in small boxes from which they took a pinch with their fingers, the Chinese used small bottles with a spoon attached to the stopper (the spoon is visible inside the red glass snuff bottle shown below right). The stopper was usually made from a different material, such as a hard stone. The tiny bottles (they are usually

*An 18th/19thC painted glass snuff bottle, painted with chicken and birds. 2.5in (6.5cm) high, E*

2–3in/5–7.5cm high) were made at the Imperial workshop for use by members of the royal family, or as gifts by them to their ministers and foreign diplomats. Eventually, however, snuff bottles were used throughout Chinese society.

*A rare Qianlong Period faceted blue glass snuff bottle. 3in (7.5cm) high F*

## Shapes and materials

Most snuff bottles were cylindrical or of flattened ovoid form, although rarer example may be elongated (see right) or facetted (see below) and were made from porcelain, lacquer, amber, coral, ivory, jade, agate and other hard stones, but most were made from glass.

## Techniques

The bottles were often carved or painted and the workmen at the Imperial workshop devised many decorative techniques. Some clear glass bottles were painted on the inside with highly detailed designs using

*A rare 18thC ruby glass snuff bottle. 2.5in (6.5cm) high, E*

*A late 19thC cameo glass snuff bottle.*
*3in (7.5cm) high, F*

enamels. This required a very small bamboo brush bent at the tip that could be pushed into the top of the bottle. This required a great deal of skill and patience – so much so that a painter could decorate only about 700 bottles before their eyesight and coordination deteriorated.

Carved Beijing glass (see p225) was enhanced by adding a foil backing to the relief decoration. The bottle shown above has foil-backed fruiting gourds on a plain turquoise ground and an agate stopper

## Colours

On Beijing glass pieces, the base glass was traditionally opaque or pearl white, clear, Imperial yellow or red. Modern pieces may use black, dark red and other colours.

The overlay glass often uses bright colours such as green, red, yellow and blue, although white and dark brown are also found. The overlay glass is usually thin so that it does not distort the shape of the bottle. Up to five colours could be used

The Qing scholar Zhao Zhiqian (1829–84) recorded that most of the snuff bottles made in Beijing in the reign of the Emperor Kangxi (1662–1722) were opaque white with blue or red decoration. Examples with cut designs were called *kehua tao liao* (cut glass overlaid objects) while those without were called *su tao liao* (plain glass overlaid objects).

*A Qianlong Period* famille rose *painted snuff bottle. 2.5in (6.5cm) high, E*

# Index

# Acknowledgements

**Alfies Antiques Market**
13–25 Church Street,
London NW8 8DT
www.alfiesantiques.com
*p217l*

**Anderson & Garland**
Crispin Court, Newbiggin Lane,
Westerhope, Newcastle upon
Tyne, Tyne and Wear NE5 1BF
www.andersonandgarland.com
*p126cl*

**Andrew Lineham Fine Glass**
19 The Mall Camden Passage,
Islington, London N1 8ED
www.antiquecolouredglass.info
*p94, p110, p112tr, p113tr, p147r,
p170, p220tl*

**Ashmore and Burgess**
10A Doddington Road,
Chatteris, Cambs PE16 6UA
www.ashmoreandburgess.com
*p71r, p76l, p76r, p77l, p77r,
p78cr, p128bl, p218tl*

**Bearnes Hampton and
Littlewood**
St Edmund's Court,
Okehampton Street, Exeter,
Devon EX4 1DU
www.bearnes.co.uk
*p21r, p41r*

**Auktionshaus Bergmann**
Möhrendorfer Straße 4,
91056 Erlangen, Germany
www.auction-bergmann.de
*p154*

**Black Horse Antiques**
29049 Garvin Rd Valley,
NE 68064, USA
www.janicelee.biz/janiceless/
Black_Horse_Antiques
*p213l, p216, p217r, p218bl*

**Bonhams**
101 New Bond Street,
London W1S 1SR
www.bonhams.com
*p83l*

**Branksome Antiques**
370 Poole Road, Branksome,
Poole, Dorset BH12 1AW
*p212l, p214tl*

**Brookside Antiques**
44 North Watter Street,
New Bedford, MA, 02740
*p185l, p185r, p208, p209l, p209r,
p214cr, p221tr, p221br*

**Bukowskis Market**
Arsenalsgatan 4, Box 1754,
11187 Stockholm, Sweden
www.bukowskis.se
*p162r, p166*

**Cheffins Fine Art**
Clifton House, 1 & 2 Clifton
Road, Cambridge, CB1 7EA
www.cheffins.co.uk
*p14, p23r*

**Craftsman Auctions**
109 Main Street, Putnam,
CT, 06260, USA
www.craftsman-auctions.com
*p189l, p199l, p199r, p201tr*

**Decodame**
853 Vanderbilt Beach Road,
PMB 8, Naples,
FL34 108, USA
www.decodame.com/antiques
*p173r*

**Dee Atkinson Harrison**
The Exchange Saleroom,
Exchange Street,
Driffield, Yorks YO25 6LD
www.dee-atkinson-harrison.
co.uk
*p85l, p87cr*

**Dorotheum**
Dorotheergasse 17,
Vienna, Austria
www.dorotheum.com
*p61l, p121cr, p122bc, p125tl,
p143tr, p156, p157l, p157r, p159l,
p174, p179l, p179r*

**Dreweatts & Bloomsbury
Auctions**
Donnington Priory Salesrooms,
Donnington,
Newbury RG14 2JE
www.dnfa.com/donnington
*p1, p17l, p24, p25l, p29l, p32, p34,
p35l, p37l, p42, p43r, p47l, p55r,
p57r, p59r, p63r, p68l, p69r, p85r,
p96, p139br, p149r*

**Duke's Auctions**
The Dorchester Fine Art
Salerooms, Weymouth Avenue,
Dorchester, Dorset DT1 1QS
www.dukes-auctions.com
*p.39b*

**DuMouchelles**
409 East Jefferson Avenue,
Detroit, MI 48226
www.dumouchelle.com
*p171l*

**Fieldings Auctioneers**
Mill Race Lane, Stourbridge,
West Midlands DY8 1JN
www.fieldingsauctioneers.
co.uk
*p19r, p22, p50, p71l, p78tl,
p78bl, p89r, p95l, p98tr, p99tc,
p100br, p120br, p132b, p165l, p169l*

**Auktionshaus Dr Fischer**
Trappensee-Schlösschen,
74074 Heilbronn, Germany
www.auctions-fischer.de
*p108, p136, p137l, p140, p141l,
p141r, p150, p153l, p167r*

**Frank Dux Antiques**
33 Belvedere, Lansdown Road,
Bath, Somerset BA1 5HR
www.antique-glass.co.uk
*p43l*

**Freeman's**
1808 Chestnut Street,
Philadelphia, PA 19103, USA
www.freemansauction.com
*p60, p68, p109l, p109r, p132r,
p133bl, p187tr, p191l, p220bl,
p222, p223bl, p226cl, p227br*

**T.W. Gaze & Son**
Diss Auction Rooms,
Roydon Road, Diss,
Norfolk IP22 4LN
www.twgaze.co.uk
*p79tr*

**Gorringes Auction House**
15 North Street, Lewes,
East Sussex BN7 2PD
www.gorringes.co.uk
*p6, p70, p72, p105cl, p146,
p162l*

**Hartleys**
Victoria Hall Salerooms,
Little Lane, Ilkley,
West Yorkshire LS29 8EA
www.andrewhartleyfinearts.
co.uk
*p83br, p129br*

**Jeffrey B. Herr Antiques, Inc.**
501 E Lehman Street,
Lebanon, PA 17046, USA
*p11*

**James D. Julia Inc.**
PO Box 830, Fairfield,
ME, 04937, USA
www.jamesdjulia.com
*p3, p81br, p97l, 98cl, p111r,
p115l, p115r, p116tl, p116br,
p120cl, p122tr, p135tr, p135bl,
p145l, p148l, p184, p193bc,
p194, p195r, p196, p197l, p198,
p200, p202, p203r, p204bl,
p220tr*

**Jeanette Hayhurst Fine Glass**
32A Kensington Church
Street, London, W8 4HA
*p25r, p26, p27l, p27r, p30, p31l,
p33r, p36, p37r, p38, p45r,
p46, p53r, p88l, p93r, p98br,
p99cr, p101l, p101r, p103l,
p165r, p169r*

**John Jesse**
160 Kensington Church Street,
London W8 4BN
*p121bl*

**Auktionshaus Kaupp**
Schloss Sulzburg,
Hauptstraße 62,
79295 Sulzburg, Germany
www.kaupp.de
*p144, p147l, p149l, p155r*

**Kunst-und Auktionshaus
W. G. Herr**
Friesenwall 35,
50672 Cologne, Germany
www.herr-auktionen.de
*p151l*

**Leslie Hindman Auctioneers**
1338 West Lake Street,
Chicago, IL,
60607, USA
www.lesliehindman.com
*p111l, p153r, p187bl, p225l,
p225r*

**Lillian Nassau**
220 East 57th Street,
New York,
NY, 10022, USA
www.lilliannassau.com
*p152l, p159r, p167l, p195l*

**Lyon & Turnbull Ltd.**
33 Broughton Place,
Edinburgh,
Midlothian EH1 3RR
www.lyonandturnbull.com
*p17r, p47r, p49l, p51l, p54, p55l,
p56, p59l, p61r, p.62, p64, p65l,
p88r, p104tl, p104bl, p106tl,
p106tr, p107tr, p107br, p126br,
p138, p139tl, p172*

**M & D Moir**
www.manddmoir.co.uk
*p148l*